BIG IDEAS FOR LITTLE KIDS

Teaching Philosophy through Children's Literature

Thomas E. Wartenberg

Rowman & Littlefield Education
A Division of
Rowman & Littlefield Publishers, Inc.
Lanham • New York • Toronto • Plymouth, UK

Published by Rowman & Littlefield Education
A division of Rowman & Littlefield Publishers, Inc.
A wholly owned subsidiary of
The Rowman & Littlefield Publishing Group, Inc.
4501 Forbes Boulevard, Suite 200, Lanham, Maryland 20706
http://www.rowmaneducation.com

Estover Road, Plymouth PL6 7PY, United Kingdom

British Library Cataloguing in Publication Information Available

Library of Congress Cataloging-in-Publication Data

Wartenberg, Thomas E.
Big ideas for little kids : teaching philosophy through children's literature / Thomas E. Wartenberg.
p. cm.
Includes bibliographical references (p.).
ISBN 978-1-60709-334-3 (cloth : alk. paper) — ISBN 978-1-60709-335-0 (pbk. : alk. paper) — ISBN 978-1-60709-336-7 (ebook)
1. Philosophy—Study and teaching (Elementary) 2. Children's literature—Study and teaching (Elementary) 3. Interdisciplinary approach in education. I. Title. B52.W378 2009
372.8--dc22

2009015581

Printed in the United States of America

For Jake,
who first showed me what young children are capable of doing, and
for Gary Matthews,
who showed me what to do with that knowledge

CONTENTS

PART III THE STORIES

PART IV IMPLICATIONS

LIST OF TABLES

PREFACE

This book contains everything necessary for teaching an introduction to philosophy class in elementary schools. It is the result of my own experience discussing philosophical issues with young children, from first to fifth graders, over the past twenty years. Since the very idea that kids are capable of taking part in a philosophical dialogue will surprise many of you, the book also explains quite carefully the rationale for discussing philosophy with them and, indeed, the importance of doing so.

My goal in introducing philosophy to young children has always been to encourage and support elementary-school classroom teachers in their efforts to bring philosophy into their classrooms. Because my hope is that this book will spur the efforts of teachers to do so, I emphasize the fact that you do not have to have a background in philosophy to become an elementary-school philosophy teacher. All you need is a genuine interest in fostering the independence, creativity, and inquisitiveness of your students—as well as patience and a sense of humor! If you possess these and are interested in introducing philosophy into your elementary-school classroom, you'll find everything you need to do so in this book.

Although I began by working with teachers to help them introduce philosophy into their classrooms, for the past decade my primary involvement has been through a course that I teach at Mount Holyoke

College in which my students teach philosophy to elementary-school children. The success that this course has achieved has surprised no one more than me. It is in part to encourage other philosophy professors to teach such courses that I have written this book, for it provides all the materials they will need to do so. Since my course is so unusual—I seriously doubt that anyone leaving a PhD program in philosophy in the United States has had any instruction in teaching such a class—I wanted to help others interested in teaching a course like it to do so.

My hope is this book will have an even wider readership than elementary-school teachers and college students, for parents and other adults may not only find the idea that their young children are natural-born philosophers intriguing, but may also discover that the mode of interacting with children discussed in this book offers them a way of deepening their relationships with their own children or those of others. So even though it is written very much as a handbook to be used in teaching philosophy to young children in a school setting, it can provide guidance for anyone interested in discussing philosophy with children.

Suggesting that philosophy should be taught in elementary schools raises many deep and controversial issues. For the most part, I have not addressed them here, lest such a discussion get in the way of the book's primary purpose of facilitating the teaching of philosophy in elementary schools. Rather than engaging in such theoretical disputes in order to convince readers of the viability of an elementary-school philosophy class, my hope is that anyone who reads this book will come to see the benefits of doing philosophy with young children by means of the practical example embodied in it.

This book, then, is intended as a guide for teaching an introduction to philosophy course in an elementary-school classroom. In the first four chapters, I explain exactly what I mean when I speak of elementary-school children *doing philosophy*. I also explain why those without any formal training in philosophy are able to facilitate philosophical discussions among young children.

In the balance of the book, I present the materials necessary for teaching an introduction to philosophy course for elementary-school children. My students and I developed these materials while teaching at the Jackson Street School in Northampton, Massachusetts; the Pioneer Valley Chinese Immersion Charter School in Hadley, Massachusetts; and the Martin Luther King Jr. Charter School of Excellence in Springfield, Massachusetts. The guiding idea of our engagement in these schools was to introduce elementary-school children to philosophy in the same systematic way that college students generally are. The course that you will find presented in this book was thus conceived as an elementary-school version of a typical college-level introduction to philosophy class. The aim was to have the young students we taught develop not only the skills necessary for doing philosophy but an awareness of what philosophy as a field of inquiry encompasses.

Our method for accomplishing this uses picture books as prompts for philosophical discussions. Our introduction to philosophy class uses eight different children's books to discuss issues in all the major fields of philosophy, from ethics to aesthetics and metaphysics to the theory of knowledge.

This book, then, is intended to serve as a jumping off place for anyone interested in acquainting young children with philosophy or—to put the point in a way more congruent with the views advanced here—in supporting the philosophical questions that young children find themselves puzzled by. Once you have been bitten by the bug of doing philosophy with children, you can find more materials for doing so at my website: teachingchildrenphilosophy.org. There you can also find more details about the course I teach to undergraduates.

There are many people whom I want to thank, for they have played a huge role in making my work with children possible. Gwen Agna, the principal of the Jackson Street School in Northampton, Massachusetts, had the foresight to see the potential of elementary-school philosophy. Mary Cowhey worked closely with me and opened up her second-grade class to me. Kimberly Gerould and the late Susan Fink also supported my work at the school. At the Martin Luther King Jr. Charter School of Excellence in Springfield, Massachusetts, Lan Katz gave me the opportunity to develop a more systematic approach to elementary-school philosophy, and my ex-student, Sulaiha Schwartz, who became a teacher at that school, made a huge effort to insure the success of the program.

At Mount Holyoke College, a number of people have helped me develop my idea of having college students teach elementary-school philosophy. Don O'Shea, the dean of the faculty, has been very supportive of my efforts. Alan Bloomgarden, the new Coordinator of Community Based Learning has also been both enthusiastic about my work and generous in his support of it. But I especially want to thank all the students who have taken my course—Philosophy 280, Philosophy for Children—for their enthusiasm and support. Without their help, and especially that of the mentors in my course over the years—Heidi Winterburn, Paula Carpentier, Chloe Martin, Kelly Albrecht, Reisa Alexander, and Ariel Sykes—not only would this book never have been written, but the whole program I have developed would not have existed. I have learned as much from them as I have taught them. Although I have revised all of the question sets included in this book, some of the original ones were developed for my website by the following students, all of whose contributions I gratefully acknowledge: Christina M. Blair, Nicole Giambalvo, Lindsay Kurahara, Melissa Saltman, Jelena Spasojevic, Ariel Sykes, and Kate Vigour.

A number of friends and colleagues have read the manuscript and given me helpful suggestions. I thank them all: Wendy Berg, Jayme Johnson, Gary Matthews, and Joe Moore. Richard Brunswick deserves thanks for helping me come up with the book's title.

The Squire Family Foundation and its director, Roberta Israeloff, provided the support I needed to have the time to develop the materials upon which this book is based. I am very grateful that Roberta and the foundation recognized the value of introducing philosophy in elementary schools and chose to support my efforts in that direction. Their recognition gave me the impetus to push ahead with this project.

The two people to whom this book is dedicated each deserve special thanks. As readers of this book will discover, my own son, Jake, played a crucial role in my discovery of the potential that young children have for philosophical thinking. Although he is now a teenager, Jake remains amazingly supportive of the project of teaching philosophy to young children. Indeed, he has spent many hours improving my website out of his conviction in the importance of introducing philosophy to children. I owe him an incredible debt of gratitude not only for his support but also for all the ways in which his philosophical inquisitiveness has enriched my life.

Gary Matthews has been extremely generous with both his time and expertise in support of my efforts. His inspiration and, indeed, ideas permeate this book. Without his model—as both a philosopher and an educator of young children—I never would have ventured into the field of philosophy for children. He, too, has enriched my life, and for this I thank him deeply.

Finally and as always, I want to thank my wife, Wendy Berg, for her support and understanding. Without her push to get involved with Jackson Street, I would not have begun the long path that led to the writing of this book. I thank her for getting me to go where I would never have dared to go without her encouragement.

1

TEACHING PHILOSOPHY IN ELEMENTARY SCHOOLS

1

NATURAL-BORN PHILOSOPHERS

As I was putting my then five-year-old son to bed one evening, he turned to me and asked, "Daddy, how did the first human get here?" Surprised by his question, I asked Jake to explain what was puzzling him. "Well," he said, "You and Mom are my parents, and Oma and Opa [his names for his paternal grandparents] are your parents. And they had parents, too. But what about the first humans? How did they get here?" Surprised at his interest in this philosophical issue, I began to discuss with him different theories that had been proposed as answers to it. By the time we were finished, if not satisfied, he was at least willing to leave the question for the time being and go to sleep.

To anyone familiar with the history of Western philosophy, it is apparent that my son had become puzzled by an issue that has bedeviled philosophers for at least 2,500 years: How could human life have begun? Jake could understand that he had come into being from my wife and me, and that each of us similarly had parents. In turn, our parents had parents, and so on. But at some point, you are confronted by an apparently insoluble dilemma: Either the series goes on forever—but how could that be, for that would mean there was an infinite number of humans prior to the present? Or there is a point at which there were two humans who did not have parents and who started the whole human race—but then, where did they come from? By what means did they spring into existence?

Of course, this is a point at which many have chosen to make reference to God, for one reason to invoke a supreme being is precisely because he has the ability to create things, including humans, from nothing. But my son has a scientific attitude toward the world, and I knew that he would resist bringing God into the picture to explain the origins of human life. Discussing evolutionary theory with him—that humans had resulted from apes through a mutation—kept him at bay for a while, although he eventually reformulated his worry about how living things could have come into existence from a nonliving universe.

Jake's questions showed me that, already at age five, he had been bitten by the bug called "philosophy," and this surprised me. There were a number of different reasons for my astonishment. First, I was genuinely amazed that Jake had been puzzled by this issue without any prompting from me. As a college teacher, I am used to having to struggle to get students to see the significance of metaphysical puzzles. Could a five-year-old child, I wondered—even one as precocious as Jake—actually have a more intuitive grasp of philosophical issues than my own college students?

I was also surprised by the tenacity with which Jake puzzled over this issue. After our nighttime conversation, he did not let the matter drop. Not only did he continue to ask more about the generation of human beings, but he also started to ask questions about related issues such as the infinitude of time and space. Once again, I was startled to realize that a five-year-old could see for himself that there was a range of related metaphysical issues all having to do with infinite sequences. Could it be, I asked myself, that young children like Jake were actually protophilosophers?

To answer this question, we need to reflect on what philosophy itself is. At its most basic level, philosophy attempts to solve fundamental puzzles about our lives and the world in which we find ourselves. The question that bothered Jake about how human life could have sprung into existence is a philosophical one. Even though scientific discoveries are relevant to our thinking about this question, it is ultimately philosophers who help us think about this abstract issue, even if they haven't yet provided a definitive solution to it. In pursuing such issues, philosophers remain puzzled by the very issue that vexed my young son as he tried to make sense of the world in which he found himself.

This suggests that philosophers are people who have never outgrown their sense that the world is a very puzzling place in which there are many questions demanding answers. For the most part, people seem generally content to follow the advice implicit in Paul's first letter to the Corinthians:

> When I was a child, I spoke as a child, I understood as a child: But when I became a man, I put away childish things (1 Cor. 13:11; cited in Barclay 2002).

Philosophers, however, retain their youthful attitude of posing questions about the world. They want things to make sense to them and refuse to drop that demand in order to simply "get on" with the business of being adults.

This image of the philosopher as an overgrown child is at odds with the venerable images of them as great bearded old men, as in, for example, Raphael's great painting *School of Athens*. From Plato onward, there has been a feeling among philosophers and, indeed, the public at large, that philosophy is appropriately pursued toward the end of one's life. The idea has been that philosophers need material on which to reflect that only a long life can supply. The hope is that with old age comes the wisdom that is taken to be characteristic of the philosopher.

This book is written with the conviction that trying to maintain philosophy as the exclusive domain of the old—or those of at least college age—is a serious mistake, one that has deep implications for our lives as human beings and for the society in which we live. As Jake's example shows, philosophy comes naturally to the young and needs to be viewed as something they can legitimately pursue, so we should foster their interest rather than snuff it out.

This belief underlies my attempt to encourage the teaching of philosophy in elementary schools. Although grade school is often thought of as a place in which young children learn basic social skills and the fundamentals of the three Rs—reading, 'riting, and 'rithmetic—focusing only on these aspects of a child's education can have disastrous consequences. The early years of schooling are the time when children first encounter organized learning, and their lifelong attitudes toward knowledge and education are indelibly formed during this period. To fail to acquaint young pupils with the joys of learning is a grave injustice that will harm them for the rest of their lives.

Because children are born with natural inquisitiveness, it is important to foster this aspect of their creativity. Schools need not so much to develop the spirit of inquiry in their young charges as to demonstrate to them that this spirit will be cultivated during their formal educations by giving their investigations direction and guidance. In order not to turn young children off to school, we need to show them that school will help them find a way to think about and resolve the questions that they naturally encounter as they grow and develop.

But it is not just children themselves who will benefit from the introduction of philosophy into elementary schools. Society as a whole will reap the benefit of having more critical, skeptical citizens who have learned not to trust authorities simply because of their social positions, but to look for evidence and reasons on their own. A democratic society can ill afford allowing its future citizens to grow up with a sense that television will provide them with all the answers they need.

In his famous dialogue *The Republic* (1961), Plato (429–347 BCE) boldly asserted that there would be no justice in the world until philosophers became kings. Here, I will make a similarly brash claim: Education will not live up to its ideals until we make every student a philosopher. Just as Plato's social vision depended upon having rulers who possessed the truth, so our own democratic society requires a citizenry of independent, critical thinkers that only a philosophical education can produce.

I am aware how idealistic this might sound to you. Especially in an age in which standardized tests are the norm, so that teachers are forced more and more to teach to what the tests will test rather than to imbue their classrooms with a genuine love of learning, is it really possible to introduce philosophy into elementary-school curricula? What sense does it make to ask our already overburdened teachers to add philosophy into an already crammed curriculum in which such traditional subjects as math and language skills have already been supplemented with multiculturalism and other important concerns?

The reason these fears are unfounded is that philosophy, as I practice it in elementary schools, is not another subject added onto the existing curriculum of language arts, mathematics, science, and so on. Instead, elementary-school philosophy is a methodology for teaching material that is already part of the standard elementary-school curriculum, especially in the language arts. Because I use children's books like Arnold Lobel's *Frog and Toad Together* (1999) and Shel Silverstein's *The Giving Tree* (1964)—books that are already widely used in elementary-school classrooms—to stimulate philosophical discussion among the children themselves, teachers do not have to figure out where philosophy fits into their crowded days. All they need to do is restructure the language-arts lessons they already teach.

Not only does using children's books to stimulate philosophical discussion allow children to articulate and substantiate their own views on such important topics as the nature of bravery (discussed in one of the stories in *Frog and Toad Together*) and the appropriate attitude to take toward other living things (raised by *The Giving Tree*) but it also enhances all the other areas of the grade-school curriculum. For example, in learning to discuss philosophical questions students will develop the sorts of language skills that most grade-school curricula emphasize. They will learn to articulate their ideas clearly, to back them up with valid reasons, and to discuss their views with others in a reasonable manner. In addition, they will learn how to assess the evidence for claims that are presented to them, rather than to simply accept what authorities—be they books or people—tell them is so. A philosophically educated nine-year-old is a more sophisticated and critical thinker than most people believe possible.

This book is intended as a guide that will enable you to teach philosophy to elementary-school children. After discussing the specific methods that I use to do so, I will go over a set of seven picture books and one chapter book that you can use to teach an elementary-school introduction to philosophy course.

I can already hear you thinking, "How can *I* teach philosophy to school children? After all, I never took any philosophy in college. I wouldn't know where to begin. Although I was interested in philosophy as a high school student, I've never been able to understand what philosophers are talking about. I know I'll never be able to teach it, intriguing as the idea might be!"

Let me reassure you: You don't have to know any philosophy to teach it! I realize that's an extraordinary statement to make, but it's absolutely true. As you will discover in reading this book, the *children* will contribute the philosophy if you only help them by teaching them how to discuss philosophical issues with one another. So don't let your own worries about not knowing much, or even any, philosophy stand in your way. You will discover what philosophy is from helping your students discuss it!

2

HOW I BECAME A CHILDREN'S PHILOSOPHY TEACHER

Perplexity is probably one of the first reactions many people have when they hear that I teach college students how to do philosophy with elementary-school children. Since philosophy is an academic subject that generally is not taught in the United States until college, it's not hard to understand this response. And given most people's notion of what philosophy is, one can easily empathize with their puzzlement at the contention that philosophy is an activity that young people not only can actually take part in at school, but already have a natural inclination toward pursuing.

When I first got involved in teaching philosophy to young children, I actually shared that skepticism and, in fact, I didn't then think that I was really teaching children how to philosophize. In my first efforts to introduce philosophy into elementary schools, I worked with teachers and thought of myself as helping them teach critical thinking, a skill or set of skills that I knew young kids really needed help acquiring. But I nonetheless used the label of teaching philosophy because that was my academic specialty, and it had a sort of cache that made teachers intrigued and interested in working with me.

So let me tell you how I got involved in this rather unusual undertaking: I had just read a book by Tracy Kidder, a well-known nonfiction writer who lives near Northampton, Massachusetts, where I also reside. The book, *Among Schoolchildren* (Kidder 1989), tells the story of Chris Zajac, a fifth-grade teacher at the Kelly School, located in nearby Holyoke, Massachusetts. Kidder has a penchant for stories about heroic individuals fighting against the odds to achieve a goal that others think of as quixotic. *Among Schoolchildren* follows that trajectory, portraying Zajac as a teacher struggling to get her pupils to succeed at school when all the factors in their environment conspired to keep them from taking education seriously, for most of Zajac's students came from backgrounds in which education was not viewed as leading anywhere and were surrounded by a peer culture that was hostile to it.

Despite my admiration for Zajac's heroic efforts, one particular feature of her teaching struck me as problematic: In order to get her pupils to focus on the lessons she wanted—whether it was spelling rules or the heinous math tables—Zajac would cajole them by threatening to withhold the treat with which she ended each day: the "read-aloud." This threat appeared to have miraculous power, for the students would quiet down and persevere with their appointed tasks, lest they jeopardize the event they seemed to relish above all else in their otherwise quite traditional school days: having their teacher read them a book.

Kidder regarded this stratagem as an example of Zajac's skill and imagination as a teacher who had to learn how to teach without support from her fellow teachers, let alone any more structured mentoring options. But to me, this tactic was almost tragic because of its failure to use children's enthusiasm for the read-aloud as a means of motivating their interest in other academic tasks and not just as icing on the cake, so to speak.

So when I began teaching philosophy to elementary-school children, I followed almost the reverse procedure to Zajac's. I began where she ended: by reading the children a story. It's true that I chose ones to read because of their philosophical content, but many children's books raise philosophical issues, so this was not much of a departure.

I might, for example, read them one of Arnold Lobel's wonderful Frog and Toad stories, such as "Dragons and Giants" or "Cookies" (both in Lobel 1999). When I was done reading the story, I would ask the kids a question about what I took to be the central philosophical concept in the story. If I'd read them "Cookies"—a story in which Frog and Toad try different tactics to keep themselves from gorging on the delicious cookies Toad has baked and thereby making themselves sick—I would focus on the idea of "will power." In the story, Frog actually defines will power as "not doing something you really want to do" (Lobel 1999, 35). Clearly, this is a paradoxical notion. If you want to do something, wouldn't you just go ahead and do it? What sense is there in saying that you have the ability not to do something that you really want to do? Well, that's a perfect place for a philosophical discussion to start, so that's exactly what I asked the kids to think about.

Later, I will show you examples that convey the enthusiasm with which the children take up such philosophical questions and begin to discuss them among themselves. For now, what matters is that I used the read-aloud not as a reward for compliant behavior, but as a means for teaching the children a variety of language-arts skills.

All too often, language arts, the term that the curriculum standards use to capture a range of linguistic and intellectual skills that teachers are supposed to teach children, is reduced to spelling and reading. But, in fact, it covers many other skills, including comprehending a text and learning to develop an argument. What's amazing about using children's literature as the focus for a philosophic discussion is that the children learn these language-arts skills almost by osmosis: They are so eager to talk about the story and share their views that they simply pick up along the way all the skills required for taking part in our discussions.

This explains why I got interested in teaching philosophy to elementary-school children and how I actually do it. I thought that teaching philosophy through children's literature was an extremely underappreciated way of getting kids to be very interested in what happens in school, to see their lessons as really fun and not something that they were interested in doing unless you threatened to withhold something that they really liked: the read-aloud. Instead, by inverting Mrs. Zajac's procedure, the philosophy read-aloud fuels the kids' curiosity and gets them to learn many skills naturally, without having to give them specific instructions like "OK, kids, now we're going to learn how to defend a position that you have against others who disagree with it," which would likely sap all of their energy and interest.

I began teaching elementary-school children philosophy, then, as a way of getting them to do what the schools wanted them to do anyway—learn language skills—but in a much more fun and exciting manner than they previously had. Soon, however, the children taught me that there is much more at stake. For, as I gained more experience working in the classroom—and as my own son got older and I had more firsthand experience with a child who was genuinely intrigued by philosophical ideas—I came to see a further and even deeper potential that was unleashed by teaching philosophy in an elementary school.

Gradually, I came to realize how puzzled children are by philosophical questions. We all know that children thrive on asking questions. "Daddy, why is the sky blue?" is the apocryphal example of the curiosity that moves young children. All too often, however, we grown-ups don't take our kids' questions seriously. In part, this is because their questions are distractions from our need to get things done. Kids are always pausing to smell the flowers—only they don't just enjoy their smell, they wonder what makes them smell sweet rather than sour or why we should find that particular smell "yummy" instead of experiencing it as "gross" or "yucky."

You probably know that the ancient Athenians put to death Socrates (469–399 BCE)—often regarded as the real founder of Western philosophy—for teaching philosophy to their young men. (Young women, I'm afraid, never had a chance to interact with him, as they were bound to their homes. And noncitizens didn't have much chance to do anything in that ancient city other than what their masters commanded.) Although philosophy professors tell the story of Socrates' trial, conviction, and punishment to show their students that philosophy is important despite social attitudes that disparage it, his story contains a very important truth that is not always emphasized: Philosophers are "pains in the butt."

When you want to proceed with a law case, the last thing you want to do is to engage in a protracted discussion about the nature of law and whether there is even such a thing as justice in the first place, as Socrates is recorded as having done in Plato's dialogue *Euthyphro* (Plato 1961). You just want to get on with the business at hand. The Athenians didn't like Socrates' practice of interrupting them when they were taking care of business, much less encouraging their kids to do the same. So, it's not really surprising that they wanted to get rid of him. (Philosophy professors also tend to ignore Socrates' refusal to be exiled as the reason that death became the only option for his punishment, but that's another story.)

One thing that philosophers have in common with children, then, is a reluctance to get on with anything until they understand why they should. My son, Jake, is an expert at this. If there's a moment of silence, it's a rare occasion when it doesn't get broken by his asking some type of hypothetical question—"Dad, if you suddenly had a lot of money, would you prefer . . ."—and the discussion is on. Or we'll be going to buy something, and he'll start asking the most interesting questions about how it works . . . only all I want to do is to get back in the car and head home. He is a pain . . . the very sort of pain that philosophers are because they are professional kids who don't take things for granted. We philosophers don't just want to get on with the task at hand; we want to ponder it for a moment and question whether it's really what we should be doing with our time. What a drag!

At least to many adults, especially parents. But to children, this is the truly wonderful thing about doing philosophy: We philosophers take kids' concerns seriously, and we let them spend time thinking through their ideas about them. And kids don't merely say "the darndest things"—as Art Linkletter (1957) once quipped—they often say the most insightful things . . . if we only would take the time to really listen to what they say. And that's exactly what philosophy for children encourages children themselves to do: to listen carefully to one another as they express their own philosophical ideas and to discuss them respectfully with each other. When this happens, the results are genuinely spectacular.

Recently, I was introducing the idea of doing philosophy to a fifth-grade class at the Jackson Street Elementary School in Northampton, Massachusetts. After some general remarks about philosophy, I told them we were going to think about a philosophical question: Why is stealing wrong? After a few comments, Matthew responded that stealing was wrong because your parents told you that it was. Jennifer's hand shot up in the air, demanding to be recognized. When I called on her, she responded, "Stealing is not wrong because your parents tell you that it is. The reason they tell you that it's wrong is because it is."

Now this may not strike you as particularly insightful, but it is precisely the argument that Socrates presents to Euthyphro, the central character in Plato's dialogue of the same name. Socrates' claim is that the rightness or wrongness of an action is an objective property of that action, so that what makes it wrong cannot be anyone's attitude toward it, even that of the gods, as the traditional Greek religion had taught. I remember spending hours trying to figure out what exactly Socrates was arguing when I took my first history of philosophy class as a junior in college—and here was a fifth grader articulating that very argument on her own! It's no surprise that, as one of my students later told me, my mouth just hung open for a moment as I realized the significance of what I had just heard.

It's uncanny how often such an experience happens when I am discussing philosophy with elementary-school children. They often have a sophisticated understanding of philosophical issues and are able to articulate it clearly in discussion with their peers. How could one not want to foster this amazing ability?

Acknowledging kids' philosophical abilities contradicts some of our most cherished views about children and childhood. In our post-Freudian era, the notion that children are innocent and incapable of deliberate cruelty no longer has much currency. Still, childhood is seen as a time in which children are supposed to learn those things necessary for them to be functioning and functional adults.

But viewing childhood this way does not accord childhood its due as a distinct life stage, with needs, desires, and capabilities of its own. As I have been arguing, childhood is a time during which many specifically philosophical issues arise that children think about a great deal. So it makes sense, even though it goes against the grain of much traditional educational theory, to allow children access to philosophy as a way of honoring what's special about their own unique stage of life.

So now, as a result of my experiences in elementary schools, I no longer think of myself as someone who only helps children acquire critical thinking skills. I view myself as an advocate of sorts, who wants to enable children to do something that comes naturally to them and at which they are astoundingly good: engage in philosophical discussions of important issues. And, as an advocate, I aim to convince you that you can do exactly what I have done. So let's turn to seeing exactly what it takes to make this happen.

3

LEARNER-CENTERED TEACHING

One of the reasons that philosophy is not widely taught at the elementary-school level is that those responsible for teaching young children generally don't think that they have the specialized knowledge or skills necessary for doing so. Certainly, if what teaching philosophy in grade school involved was explaining philosophical claims such as why Descartes (1596–1650) thought that all our ordinary beliefs about the world might actually be false, this view would be justified (Descartes 1993). Ironically, one of my best students was excited by this very possibility when she heard that I would be offering a course in teaching philosophy in elementary schools. To her, the thought of explaining Descartes and Kant to young kids was really exciting, and she was very disappointed to discover that that was not what we would be doing.

Almost everyone else will be relieved to discover that teaching philosophy to elementary-school children does not involve giving lectures on the great philosophers of the past or the central problems of Western philosophy. So, then, what exactly does doing philosophy with elementary-school children involve?

Our focus when teaching philosophy in elementary-school classrooms is giving children the opportunity to discuss philosophical questions among themselves. As I have already explained, young children are natural-born philosophers. What we do is give them the chance to pursue their natural inclination for philosophy in the formal setting of the classroom by initiating discussions of basic questions about human life and a world whose mysteries children are just discovering and trying to make sense of.

But, in doing so, we don't tell them what to think about anything; our only purpose is to assist the children so that they can have a productive discussion with one another. For even though young children may be natural-born philosophers, they are not born ready to discuss issues with their peers. *That's* what we have to teach them how to do.

Because "all" that the teacher has to do is to assist the children in *their* philosophical discussion, it doesn't require any special philosophical knowledge to teach elementary-school philosophy. All you need to know is how to facilitate a philosophical discussion among your students.

It's important to realize that there is a model of what teaching involves that makes it difficult to see how an elementary-school teacher could possibly teach her students philosophy, what I call the *teacher-centered model of learning*. The goal of teaching, on this view, is the students' *acquisition of knowledge*. This seems so self-evident a goal for learning that it can be hard to think about it critically. After all, children do lack a great deal of the knowledge that most adults have—such as how to spell, read, and add. Isn't the point of education to provide them with the knowledge they lack, to transform them, at least eventually, from ignorant youngsters into knowledgeable adults?

Once teaching is conceived of in this way, many features of the teacher-centered model follow. The *teacher*, as the *possessor* of the desired knowledge, must *transmit* her knowledge to her *ignorant pupils*. Since the students are ignorant, the teacher must *control* the process of knowledge acquisition at every step. Who else is there to ensure that the children are progressing from a state of ignorance to one of knowledge?

Even the emphasis on testing follows from this view. The way to tell whether a student has acquired the knowledge he must is to require him to (re)produce it. And what, after all, is a test but a situation designed to compel students to spill out for the teacher those things she has decided they need to know?

Perhaps the most striking features of the teacher-centered model is the centrality it accords to the teacher in the educational process. Not only does she have the knowledge that the students lack, but she sets the agenda for learning and she transmits her knowledge to each student in a manner that she determines. But almost as striking is the assumption that children will simply fit into the role of pliant learner that this model creates for them. Rather than seeing children as independent beings with needs and desires of their own, this model conceives children as empty receptacles, ready to accept whatever the teacher has determined is good for them.

Clearly, if we apply this model to teaching philosophy to children, it becomes clear why an elementary-school teacher would think she was incapable of teaching philosophy to her students. Because elementary-school teachers generally lack any specialized knowledge about the discipline of philosophy, they would be unable to teach it, for the teacher-centered model requires that the teacher possess a supply of knowledge that she can distribute to her charges. Given the prevalence of this model of learning and teaching, it's not surprising that there is so much skepticism about the possibility of teaching philosophy in elementary schools.

But philosophy *can* be taught to elementary-school children, as I can amply testify to from my own experience and from watching the classroom practices of the teachers I have worked with. And one of the reasons for this is that, as we have seen, children are *natural-born philosophers*. That is, as they attempt to make sense of the often perplexing and sometimes confusing world in which they find themselves, children just naturally ask questions that are decidedly philosophical, as Jake did when he wondered how the first human came into being.

So when we teach children philosophy—and this method is suitable to other subjects as well—we seek to mobilize their natural curiosity and help them *discover, express, and support* their own answers to questions that concern them. For this reason, I call this method of education *learner-centered teaching* to emphasize the centrality it accords to the children as natural investigators and learners. (For a comparison of the teacher-centered and learner-centered models, see table 3.1)[1]

The fundamental assumption of learner-centered teaching is that the student, no less than the human mind itself, is not simply a tabula rasa (blank tablet) upon which anything a teacher wants can be inscribed. Instead, it recognizes that the student-learner has many dispositions,

Table 3.1. Two Models of Learning

Teacher-Centered Learning	*Learner-Centered Teaching*
Goal: Acquisition of knowledge	Goal: Students' development, articulation, and support of their own views
Students: Ignorant	Students: Naturally inquisitive
Teacher: Possessor of knowledge	Teacher: Facilitates investigation
Knowledge transmitted through dyadic student-teacher relation	Learning happens through group investigation
Teacher sets the agenda	Students determine the course of the investigation
Use of testing	Dialogue itself as evidence of its success

capacities, and ideas that education must acknowledge. This means that, among other things, for education to be successful, the student must have a desire to participate in the process of learning itself. All too often, this doesn't happen since that process is completely controlled by someone else. Part of what makes learner-centered teaching different is that the learner is able to exert control over his own learning. Although the teacher still has an important role to play, she no longer is the sole author of the learning process.

In transferring children's natural curiosity to the classroom, the main innovation we make is that of transforming the child's investigation of the world from an individual process into a social or group one. If we step away from the classroom and recognize that learning is something that takes place throughout our lives in very different contexts and settings, it becomes apparent that very little *real learning* takes place individually; for the most part, it is the combined efforts of people working together that have solved all the problems that the human race has actually faced. Only a Robinson Crusoe—marooned alone on his island—confronts the world on his own. When we human beings work together to solve our problems, we find that we are a remarkably capable species. Despite the wealth of problems that we have to face, we take the optimistic view that we can solve them all so long as we work together.

The learner-centered model of teaching attempts to create a classroom that takes account of the nature of individual learners and the social situation of the classroom in which they find themselves. It seeks to engage students communally in a natural way, so that they will be motivated to work together to solve problems that they themselves actually encounter and, hence, want to find solutions to. Those solutions get worked out through trial-and-error processes that the group undertakes together, and learning results when the children take part in them.

Since children are not generally used to treating learning as a *group* project, they need the teacher to facilitate their interactions with each other in such a way that they engage cooperatively and supportively in an attempt to answer a question that puzzles them. The teacher is a guide who oversees the students' own process of problem solving to ensure that it proceeds in accordance with norms that make it possible for the children to work together cooperatively.

Because the dialogue that emerges from this process of joint investigation is itself evidence that learning is taking place—or failing to—there is no need for imposing a punitive style of assessment on the learning process. The success of an investigation can simply be registered through a careful examination of the discussion itself as well as by the students' own reflection on it.

This, then, is the learner-centered model of teaching. Many classroom teachers already aspire to the creation of learner-centered classrooms. My goal has been to demonstrate that such classrooms are hospitable environments for philosophical discussions.

There are two problems that immediately confront anyone in introducing learner-centered teaching into her classroom. The first is how to interest the children in the philosophical issue you want to have them discuss. I call this the *initiation problem*. It is a significant issue, for the learner-centered approach to teaching requires that the questions students face arise naturally through their experience.

The second—the *regulation problem*—concerns how the teacher should oversee the group's problem solving so that it is likely to produce an outcome that is satisfactory for all of the children. The fact is, children have to be taught how to work together cooperatively. As a result, we are faced with the question of whether it is possible for someone without a background in philosophy to help children productively engage in a philosophical discussion.

I've already said that I use children's literature, especially picture books but also chapter books, as the basis for developing philosophical discussions among elementary-school children. What I now need to explain is how using stories solves both of the problems that arise in learner-centered teaching. I will discuss the initiation problem now, reserving a discussion of the regulation problem until the next chapter.

To show you how children's books can solve the initiation problem, I will first tell you another story about my son, Jake. One day Jake, then in first grade, came home upset. Apparently, the fifth graders had baked some cookies, and only the fourth graders had been invited to a party to eat them. "That's really unfair," Jake told me. "The older kids always get all the good things," he complained. "What do you mean?" I asked. He responded by telling me that all the special treats were given to the fourth and fifth graders, such as field trips and special assemblies. "It's not fair that the younger kids don't get any of those things," he concluded.

In our psychological age, I imagine that many parents would use this as an opportunity to commiserate with their child, to reassure him in some way. But, being a philosopher, I saw Jake's distress as an opportunity to initiate a philosophical conversation with him. So I asked him a question. "Jake," I queried, "what makes this unfair? After all, someday you'll be an older kid and have the same privileges as the fourth and fifth graders do now. Why isn't it all right to give different aged children different privileges so long as the younger children will eventually get the privileges now accorded to the older ones?"

Jake pondered this for a while and responded, "But what if I'm not in school here then? It's not fair to make us little kids wait until later to be treated fairly. It needs to happen now." Our conversation continued for some time, as we discussed whether it was all right to allow one group special privileges or whether justice demanded that everyone be treated exactly in the same way all of the time. The discussion ended with Jake determined to write a note to the principal demanding justice for first graders!

I tell this story to illustrate two things. First, when a child has a genuine concern, he wants to engage in discussion about it. Coming to terms, as they are, with a wealth of different phenomena, children frequently encounter things that bother them. Often they raise their concerns with the adults to whom they are closest. Although we adults rarely follow up on the opportunities these conversations provide, we need to recognize that children's need to figure out their world gives us many chances to have philosophical discussions with them. When we do so, the children are motivated to take part in the discussion precisely because they are the ones who have initiated it. In fact, they usually are very grateful that the adults to whom they are closest are taking their concerns seriously by engaging them in a discussion about *their* issues.

Second, my encounter with Jake illustrates how a carefully posed question can transform a child's feeling of distress into the motivation for a philosophical discussion. This is because a child in distress is often not simply looking to an adult for comfort. What he desires is a way to think about why he is upset and what he should do to alleviate it. Because Jake was confident that the philosophical discussion I had with him might help him figure out how to resolve his issue, he was very willing to expend a great deal of energy in engaging in a philosophical discussion with me.

Having a discussion with children after reading them a story from a picture book shares both of these two crucial features of my discussion with Jake. Because aspects of the stories that we read to the children have puzzling or bothersome features in them, the children are not simply glad to have the stories read to them. They find themselves perplexed about some issues raised by the stories. Stories about animals who call themselves brave yet run terrified from every danger they encounter ("Dragons and Giants" [Lobel 1999]) or a judge of an art contest who declares a painting of a dog bad just because she dislikes dogs (*Emily's Art* [Catalanotto 2001]) are examples of stories that engage children because they have puzzling, bothersome, or even paradoxical aspects to them. As a result, children jump at the chance to resolve the puzzles in them. The questions that we ask the children focus on these problematic aspects of the stories and give the children an opportunity to resolve their confusions.

Using a read-aloud to begin a philosophical discussion, then, solves the initiation problem in a neat way. For what we do, once the read-aloud is over, is ask the children a question that points out a philosophical puzzle in the story itself. Because the children have been engaged by the story, they naturally attempt to resolve the issue we raise. Our belief is that this process will stimulate a genuine investigation by the children into the problem or puzzle that we present because it is an issue that arises directly out of the story that they have been read.

Because many of the stories we use pose but do not resolve philosophical questions (such as whether a person who appears to be brave because he does something very dangerous can really be doing something quite stupid), a well-formulated question makes explicit a puzzle that any child will at least be wondering about implicitly after hearing the story. As a result, the children's pleasure at being read to can be redirected into a lively and engaging discussion of a philosophical problem.

It is important to emphasize that one of the basic principles of all philosophical discussion is that disagreement is not only not a problem but something to be valued, so long as it is expressed in a respectful manner. This is crucial, because philosophical issues generally do not have agreed upon solutions. For example, philosophers disagree about the answer to the question, "What is the meaning of life?" and even whether it is possible to answer it. So the point of discussing philosophical questions is *not* to learn what the correct answer is, for many do not have universally accepted answers. Rather, what we expect the children to acquire is a set of cognitive skills that allow them to decide what their own answers to such questions are and why these answers make sense.

Traditional classrooms come closest to having philosophical discussions when they employ debates about controversial issues, for children are then asked to support their views with good reasons. But in philosophy discussions, the emphasis is not on facts but defending what you think by providing good reasons for thinking what you do.

The reason, then, that children's books provide such a good means for initiating philosophical discussions is that they present philosophical issues in a way that engages the children that naturally leads to animated conversations. When we look at the actual books that we use, you will see how well they can serve to initiate philosophical discussions.

Using children's books to initiate philosophical discussions has another important advantage. Because elementary-school teachers are already using these books, they are already familiar with them and do not have to study new materials in order to teach philosophy. When we say that we are teaching children *philosophy*, we don't mean that we are *adding* a new subject into the curriculum. What we are doing is using books that teachers already are supposed to teach, but in a new and innovative manner, one that will engage the children and allow them to develop important cognitive skills.

As I've said, I will discuss how our method of teaching solves the regulation problem in the next chapter. Let me conclude the present discussion by emphasizing that the read-aloud serves to initiate a philosophical discussion in which the teacher is not the center of attention but the facilitator to a child-centered discussion among peers. Although this has generally been referred to as the creation of a community of inquiry by philosophers interested in discussing philosophical issues with children (see, for example, Kennedy 1996), I prefer to talk of learner-centered teaching because this emphasizes how the teacher should conceive of her role: as the facilitator of a learning process that takes place through the interaction of the students with one another.

Because the story remains present as the subject on which the discussion is focused, it provides the facilitator with an easy means of keeping the discussion on track. She can simply remind the children what they are supposed to be talking about, thereby refocusing the discussion in a useful way.

NOTES

1 The contrast between teacher-centered learning and learner-centered teaching is my way to describe a distinction that many others have made. See, for example, Paulo Freire's discussion of the banking conception of education (1970) for one attempt to characterize two different approaches to learning.

4

THE "GAME" OF PHILOSOPHY

In the last chapter, I said I would discuss what I called the regulation problem, that is, how a teacher could facilitate a philosophical discussion among children that was likely to produce a good outcome. This problem is especially acute since most teachers are not experts in philosophy. We have already seen that it is possible for a teacher to lead such a discussion because he is not expected to transmit his specialized knowledge of significant philosophical ideas or theories, a task that he is probably not prepared to undertake. Instead, his role is to facilitate a philosophical discussion among his students in which the students work out among themselves their own answer(s) to philosophical questions stemming from a story that has just been read to them. But how, exactly, is a teacher supposed to oversee such a discussion?

A first problem is that a teacher may not have a clear idea of what makes a question or issue philosophical. This is actually one of the most difficult philosophical questions that there is, one that philosophers disagree about vehemently. My view is that a question is philosophical when it is one that cannot be answered empirically and for which no specific discipline has been developed that is capable of providing an answer to it.

Consider, for example, the paradigmatic child's question I mentioned earlier, "Daddy, why is the sky blue?" This is not a philosophical question because there is a well-established way to go about answering it. Physicists, beginning with John Tyndall in 1859, determined that air molecules scatter blue light from the sun in such a way as to produce the blue color of "the sky." Because this is an issue within the purview of physicists, it is not a philosophical question. But if a child were to ask whether the sky really is an object that is above us, that would be a philosophical question, for it goes beyond the bounds of physics by asking about the relationship between our ordinary concepts—of which "the sky" is one—and our best scientific understanding of the ultimate constituents of the world.

Or, consider the question, Could all of my perceptual beliefs be wrong? If anything is a philosophical question, this is, for no other discipline sees it as a *real* issue for it to settle. But philosophers do. And it's also a question that comes up in most people's lives at some time or other, say when they've just woken from a particularly convincing dream and are puzzled by whether what they thought just happened really did. The crucial feature that makes this a *philosophical* question is that there is no established discipline—other than philosophy itself—to turn to in deciding how to find an answer to it. You can't ask a friend or conduct an experiment; your friend's opinion can't settle the matter for *you*, and what sort of experiment could possibly tell *me* whether or not the screen upon which the words I am typing appear is real?

This conception of philosophy also explains why many questions that appeared to be philosophical at some point in time are now recognized as not being genuinely philosophical. A good example of such a question is, What are the ultimate constituents of the universe? The ancient Greek philosophers proposed many different answers to this question—starting with water and proceeding through many different alternatives, including atoms!—but we now recognize this as a scientific question that should be settled by scientific theorizing and experimentation. Only those questions for which there is no such agreed upon discipline that provides the method for their solution count as genuinely philosophical.

When philosophers attempt to answer a question that is clearly within their realm, they try to persuade others of the correctness of their view by discursive means alone. They don't threaten each other or yell or do anything but explain their view in a way that is intended to convince people who don't yet agree with them. So, to return to the question about whether all our perceptual beliefs could be false, philosophers adopt different strategies to answer it. Many philosophers will present an argument that purports to show that not all of their perceptual beliefs can be erroneous. Others will try to prove the contrary. Still others will try to explain why it's a mistake to even try to answer the question, because the query itself relies on some false presuppositions. The philosophical strategies for dealing with philosophical questions are quite numerous, but all involve the attempt to *persuade* others discursively.

It is precisely because of philosophy's character as a discipline involving linguistic persuasion that you don't have to despair about facilitating a philosophical discussion among young children. There is some pretty widespread agreement among philosophers about how they should go about conducting their arguments, even though they disagree about nearly everything else.

To help you understand this, I want to introduce an analogy between a philosophical discussion and a game. There are, of course, all sorts of games, from chess to baseball and even so-called war games. One thing that all of these games have in common is a set of *rules* that explain which *moves* are allowed in the game and which are prohibited.

Most everyone knows that "three strikes and you're out" is a rule of baseball. Although it may seem odd to describe it this way, this rule stipulates how, after a specific event has occurred—a pitcher's throwing a third strike—there results a specific *move* in the game of baseball, namely, the batter being "out." When this situation occurs, the batter can no longer continue batting, so either a new player must come up to bat or the teams need to change places—the two alternative moves that are prescribed by the rules once a batter has had three strikes called on him, depending on the prior state of the game.

There are many other rules that together make up the game of baseball. I am asking you to think of these rules as specifying what the permissible moves within the game of baseball are. Once you adopt this perspective, it will not be hard to see that it is the *umpire's* job to *apply* the rules—to determine when a particular rule applies—so that it is clear what the next move of the game will be.

When, for example, an umpire decides whether a ball hit into the stands is fair or foul, he is deciding whether the next move of the game is adding a run to the batter's team—the result of a home run—or returning the batter to the plate, possibly with an extra strike. The umpire makes judgments about the actions of the players, determining whether their attempted moves are legitimate or not. Baseball's famed "rhubarbs," or heated arguments, often take place when team members think the umpire has made a mistake in applying the rules. What they are disputing is what move of the game should be next.

Although you might think that all of this would be a lot clearer if I used chess as my example of a game, I want you to see that the idea of a game with prescribed moves is so general that it applies to all sorts of activities that might not at first seem to be aptly described in this way. Once you accept this idea, you will be able to think of a *philosophical discussion* as a gamelike activity that is regulated by *rules*. And that will allow you to recognize that the teacher overseeing such a discussion has a natural role: the umpirelike role of making sure the rules are being correctly followed during a philosophical discussion.

In this analogy, the teacher's role is to decide whether a given *move in the game of philosophy* is legitimate or not. Like the umpire in a game of baseball, he mostly allows the players to get on with playing the game, generally stepping in only when necessary to make it clear that a particular move is a violation of a rule. Of course, like an umpire whose "Play ball!" gets a baseball game started, the teacher will have to initiate a philosophical discussion in his classroom and even make sure that it keeps moving along.

I imagine that something else may still be bothering you. After all, umpires in baseball do have to have a lot of knowledge of the rules of baseball. They need to know, for example, what happens when a fly ball hits the foul pole, as it did in a recent Red Sox game I was watching. (It actually turned out that the line on the fence didn't line up with the foul pole, causing a huge controversy. This shows that the rules have to be followed very carefully in setting up the structure in which the game takes place!) So what about the teacher who is facilitating a philosophical discussion among his elementary-school children? Doesn't he have to have a lot of specialized knowledge about the rules of philosophical discussion in order to serve as the umpirelike facilitator of the discussion?

Well, yes and no. That is, while the teacher has to have *some* knowledge of how a philosophical discussion is to be conducted, he doesn't have to have extensive knowledge of the specific philosophical topic being discussed. That's because the basic rules that specify allowable moves in a philosophical discussion are pretty simple, hard as that may be to believe.

In fact, I think there are only *six basic rules* for conducting a philosophical discussion. Although the situation can get quite complex when you try to decide how the rules apply in a particular context, it is easy for a teacher to get a handle on them, especially if he keeps in mind the basic analogy between philosophical discussions and games. For the essential point the "umpire" of a philosophical discussion has to consider is whether what a child says contributes to the ongoing discussion or hinders it, is an allowable move in the game or is against the rules and blocks the game's progress. The role of the teacher as facilitator is exactly analogous to that of the umpire: determining when a rule has been broken and stepping in to call a "penalty" that gets the game back on track.

What, then, are the essential rules for, or elements of, a philosophical discussion? As I've said, I think there are six basic ones, and they all stipulate appropriate responses that can be made at a given stage in the discussion. Don't forget that in addition to his role as facilitator, the teacher actually has another role: He also *initiates* the discussion by reading the story and asking a question. However, once the discussion proper begins, virtually all of the teacher's actions function to *regulate* the "playing" of the game of philosophy.

Here, then, are the six rules for having a philosophical discussion. What they specify are the "moves" that one is allowed to make in the game of philosophy.

1. State your position on an issue—that is, answer a question that has been asked—in a clear manner after taking time to think.

This rule may be harder to follow than you might think. In a classroom discussion, children often want to talk, even if they don't really have a relevant contribution to make. It is important to encourage the children to "think before they speak," rather than simply raising their hand.

Children also have to be taught how to express their ideas in a manner that lets other people, especially their peers, know exactly what they have in mind. So, if you don't have a clear understanding of exactly what a child has said, you need to make sure that she rephrases her ideas in a way that you can understand. Here, it's often helpful to turn to the other children and ask them if they understand what was said. After all, it is *their* discussion, so they need to understand what's been said if they are to take part in it. Any time the children make it clear that they don't understand something, you have a good reason as facilitator to ask for clarification. Hopefully, as you work with the children, they will themselves internalize the need to understand what has been said and take over this task themselves.

2. *Figure out if you* agree or disagree *with what has been said.*

Although we often know exactly what we think about an ordinary, everyday issue, the abstractness of some philosophical issues makes it hard to know what we think about *them*. It's therefore important to help the children figure out their positions on the philosophical issue being discussed.

This may require that children ask questions about what has been said, for this additional information may help them decide what they think. But an important move in the game of philosophy is determining what you think about something that someone else has said. It's therefore useful for you to ask, in response to a child's answer to a question, "Who agrees and who disagrees with what Shaquille has said?" (Again, it's important to first be sure that everyone knows what it is that Shaquille has said.) In fact, it can be very helpful to explicitly get the children to say, before they make any comment, "I agree [or disagree] with what Shaquille has said."

3. *Present a real example of the abstract issue being discussed.*

Philosophical claims are abstract and general. As part of the process of discussing them, it is very helpful to have the children give an example of the claim in question. For example, if you are discussing bravery—a topic that figures prominently in one of the stories in our elementary-school introduction to philosophy, "Dragons and Giants" (Lobel 1999)—it can be very helpful to begin the discussion by asking the children to tell everyone about a time when they were brave. This brings the story and its ideas directly into their own lives and therefore helps them see the relevance of philosophy.

However, there is a pitfall here: Children love to tell stories, so it's important to keep their contributions brief. Make sure to establish the allowable parameters for their answers before asking them to tell their stories.

4. Present a counterexample to a claim that has been proposed.

In answering a philosophical question, one often makes a general claim. For example, if you ask what makes a person brave, a child might say, "Not being scared when you do something dangerous." This is a general claim, for it says that only when a person faces dangers without fear do her actions count as brave.

An important aspect of doing philosophy is thinking about whether such general claims apply across the board to all instances of the phenomenon being discussed. And one way to show that they do not is to provide a counterexample, that is, an instance of something (bravery, in this case) that does not satisfy the criterion being advanced (facing something dangerous without fear). It's important to teach the children this skill, for it is central to how they need to assess the validity of general claims.

A good way to do so is to ask the group, after a child has presented a general claim, if they can think of circumstances when that claim does not apply or examples that do not fit it. Here, you might ask, "Can anyone think of someone who is being brave but who is not facing something dangerous without being scared?" A child might respond by telling you about something she did that she thought was brave, but admit that she was really scared when she did it, or else give you an example of someone who she thinks is brave but was really scared, too. If the children do either of these things, then they have provided a counterexample to the general claim. This would show that the proposed definition of bravery is not valid as an account of what bravery is.

A counterexample is sort of like the "Go to jail!" card in the game of Monopoly. It sends you away from the position you have reached and requires that you do something special to proceed. To get out of "jail," the children need to think about how to respond to the counterexample. They can put forward a completely different claim, taking the discussion along a different path, or they can revise the previous claim in the way I will now describe.

5. Put forward a revised version of a claim in light of criticism.

Philosophers are stubborn folks. They don't easily give up their views. As a result, when faced with a counterexample to a claim, they often put forward a revised version of it, one that "takes care of" the counterexample. So it's important that the children learn this skill as well.

Faced with a counterexample to a child's definition of bravery, you might turn to her and ask her—as well as her discussion partners—whether she, or any of them, has a way of responding to the counterexample. In our example, a student might respond by saying that you're being brave if you don't let your fears keep you from doing what you want in a dangerous situation. This would be a reformulation of the initial account of bravery that disarms the counterexample.

6. Support your position with reasons.

In the game of philosophy, it's not enough to say what you think. You have to explain *why* you think it. Children can learn to do this quite easily. After all, they ask you *Why?* so often that they don't mind being asked *Why?* themselves. The problem is making it clear what types of answers count as good philosophical reasons for why you think what you do.

A philosophical explanation has to be *logical* and provide a *good explanation* of why anyone should accept the claim. If a child is asked to explain why she thinks that, for example, bravery means acting despite one's fears, and the child responds that she read it in a book or saw it on the Web or her big sister told her so, that's not an appropriate move in the philosophy game; these are not good reasons unless they can be backed up by something more. A good reason might involve explaining what is involved in being brave, how it's an appropriate response in dangerous situations, and what role fear plays.

Students may not be able to give complete explanations for their ideas right off the bat, for this is a move that takes some practice. When a student doesn't know what to say, it's generally helpful to turn to her peers and ask them if anyone can help out by providing a good reason for the claim in question.

In a nutshell, these are the six rules (summarized in table 4.1) that are necessary for regulating a philosophical discussion. Your task as a philosophical facilitator, like that of any referee, is to make sure that people are playing by the rules as well as to keep the game progressing so that

Table 4.1. Rules for Doing Philosophy

1. State your position on an issue—that is, answer a question that has been asked—in a clear manner after taking time to think.
2. Figure out if you *agree or disagree* with what has been said.
3. Present a real example of the abstract issue being discussed.
4. Present a counterexample to a claim that has been proposed.
5. Put forward a revised version of a claim in light of criticism.
6. Support your position with reasons.

the children remain engaged by it. When the teacher is conceived as an umpire rather than a knowledge dispenser, the notion of leading a philosophical discussion will seem a whole lot easier.

Earlier, I said that when we "teach" children philosophy, we don't actually *teach* them anything but only get them to discuss their own ideas in a carefully regulated manner. Actually, I was not being completely honest with you. While we don't prescribe what the children say about anything, we do actually require that what they say fits into the rules for having a philosophical discussion that I have just spelled out. But this means that we are actually teaching them something: *How to take part in a philosophical discussion.*

The fact is, acquiring this crucial skill will benefit them in all sorts of ways in their educations and, indeed, in their lives. That's because the rules for having a *philosophical* discussion are actually the basic rules for thinking about anything at all and therefore form the basis for all the thinking that we do, no matter what we are thinking about. That's why philosophy can be characterized as the discipline that thinks about thinking, though there is more to philosophy than that.

This also helps explain why teaching children philosophy is so important. Getting children to master the rules for having a philosophical discussion provides them with some of the most basic skills they will need no matter what else they go on to study. So as well as allowing them to discuss issues and questions that really matter to them, philosophy also provides them with an important set of cognitive and behavioral skills that will be applicable throughout their educations.

When I was working with Mary Cowhey, a teacher at the Jackson Street School, we developed a set of questions to use in discussing William Steig's *The Real Thief* (2007). This is the story of a goose that is wrongly convicted of a crime on the basis of circumstantial evidence. When the students discussed the story, they wanted to understand how a person could be convicted of a crime that he didn't do on the basis of certain evidence.

To help her explain this, Mary brought in my wife, a lawyer, to explain different standards of evidence to the children. My wife explained the difference between direct and circumstantial evidence, along with the different degrees of credibility each has. This enabled the children to understand how a miscarriage of justice was possible when circumstantial evidence is the sole basis for a conviction.

As a result of these discussions, the idea of evidence became so powerful that, no matter what the students were studying—from history to science—they kept demanding to know what the evidence for any proposed claim was. Other visitors to this classroom left amazed that second graders were demanding that they support what they were saying with *evidence*, for the children were no longer willing to accept their stories at face value. (See Cowhey 2006, 157.) This is a real example of how useful a philosophical education can be in creating young children as independent thinkers.

More generally, teaching children how to have a philosophical discussion will change the culture of a classroom in a positive way. As they learn to see one another as partners in a quest for understanding, they will come to value their classmates not only as fellow knowledge seekers in the game of philosophy, but also as suitable conversation partners on virtually any topic. Children who have become skillful players of the game of philosophy will bring their new-found abilities to bear on every aspect of their schooling.

II

PREPARING TO TEACH

5

THE ELEMENTARY-SCHOOL INTRODUCTION TO PHILOSOPHY COURSE

As I've mentioned a number of times, this book contains all the materials you need to teach an introduction to philosophy course to elementary-school children. So, it's high time that I give you a better sense of what such a course involves.

The course that I am about to describe is one that my undergraduate students have taught at the Martin Luther King Jr. Charter School of Excellence in Springfield, Massachusetts. It evolved from my work there as well as with children and teachers at the Jackson Street School in Northampton, Massachusetts. The course is thus based in my actual experience and that of my students in teaching philosophy to elementary-school children. Although we have taught every grade from first to fifth, most of our recent experience has been with second and third grades. But all of the books included in the course can be taught in any grade, so long as you explain to students who have already read the books that what you are doing with the books is different from what they might be used to.

To begin, I have to say something more specific about philosophy in order to explain the actual content of this elementary-school introduction to philosophy course. Philosophy is the intellectual discipline that considers the most basic questions of human existence. The tradition of philosophizing that we will be invoking—"Western" philosophy—began in Greece in the fifth century BCE. Although philosophy is therefore two and a half millennia old, its basic questions remain the same: What can we know? What should we do? What does it all mean? But even though these questions remain without definitive solutions, philosophy has progressed in the sense that it renews our ability to reflect upon these questions in the ever-changing world in which we live.

Philosophical inquiry is generally divided into a number of specific fields (see table 5.1). Although I will provide somewhat more detailed explanations of these fields later in the book, I will give a provisional account now in order to explain the structure of our course. First, there is *metaphysics*, the philosophical discipline that considers the nature of existence. This is the headiest field of philosophy, the hardest one to get a handle on. Basically, metaphysicians wonder about what the structure of reality is really like. They ask questions such as whether the world as it appears to us is the real world and whether many of its features—like colors, smells, time, numbers—might just be projections of our human ways of thinking and perceiving.

Epistemology (from the Greek word for knowledge, *episteme*) focuses on the nature of human knowledge. The central figure for the epistemologist is the skeptic, who denies that certain accepted modes of knowing really give us knowledge. The most venerable forms of skepticism are skepticism about the reality of the external world, which asks, Do we have knowledge that there is a world external to ourselves that resembles our impressions of it? and skepticism about the existence of other minds, which poses the question, Can we be sure that, attached to

Table 5.1. The Basic Fields of Philosophy

Philosophical Field	*Basic Question*
Metaphysics	What really exists?
Epistemology	What can we know?
Philosophy of language	How does language refer to reality?
Philosophy of mind	Is the mind distinct from the body?
Ethics	How should we act?
Social and political philosophy	How should society by organized?
Aesthetics	What is art?

the bodies that we see surrounding us that behave much as we do, there are minds like our own?

A field of philosophy that came into existence only in the twentieth century is the *philosophy of language*. Prior to that time, philosophers had not given language much attention, thinking of it as simply the medium in which we expressed our thoughts, the mental items whose nature they investigated. But beginning in the early twentieth century, philosophers began to suspect that language had a much greater impact on our thinking than had previously been thought. Philosophers of language investigate the nature of language and how it enables us to effectively communicate with one another. They wonder, for example, whether language is inherently social and whether its structure determines our sense of what there is in the world, so that different languages present their users with different world pictures.

The human mind is one of the most amazing features of the world, but also one of its most puzzling. The *philosophy of mind* poses questions about the nature of the mind, such as what relation it bears to the human body. In general, it seeks to explain the nature of all mental phenomena, including thoughts, emotions, and volitions. In so doing, the philosophy of mind brings to bear the amazing results of recent research in cognitive science that may have the potential to solve the "riddle of consciousness" and to transform our self-understanding.

Ethics is the field of philosophy that addresses questions of human conduct. People generally understand that there is a difference between doing what they feel like at a given moment and what they think they *ought* to do. Ethics attempts to explain the nature of the obligation we feel to do the moral or the "right" thing. Ethicists worry about such questions as whether we have an obligation to treat other people respectfully simply by virtue of their humanity and, if so, exactly how such an obligation can be justified.

While ethics is concerned with individual human beings, the related field of *social and political philosophy* focuses on the nature of society. Foremost among its issues is the justification for government. All of the political disagreements between liberals and conservatives are reflected at a more abstract level in disputes in social and political philosophy. Some would argue, for example, that justice demands that everyone have a socially agreed upon minimum level of welfare, while others reject that contention for requiring untoward intervention into people's individuals rights.

Aesthetics focuses on questions that arise concerning art. The issues that bedevil each of the other fields of philosophy find their own specific register in aesthetics. For example, one of the most vexed issues facing the philosophy of art is the metaphysical one of exactly what distinguishes works of art from other things in the world. Since artists now include virtually everything *including* the kitchen sink in their works, the question of what makes a work of art a unique type of entity becomes more pressing. But there are also epistemological and ethical questions that get raised about art, such as whether good art can be objectionable from a moral point of view.

Another recent addition to the domain of philosophy is *environmental philosophy*. Given the widespread assumption that human beings have wrought serious damage to the natural world, philosophers have begun to question whether there is an appropriate way for humans to relate to their environment. Reacting against an earlier age's assumption that natural things were simply there for human beings to use, some philosophers argue that humans need to regard natural things as having rights of their own that must be respected.

Since a college-level introduction to philosophy course would introduce students to at least some of the above-mentioned fields of philosophy, we have decided to do the same in our elementary-school introduction to philosophy course. With this aim in mind, I chose eight books out of a virtually unlimited supply of picture books that can be used to initiate philosophical discussions with young children. With one exception, we have limited ourselves to picture books. This is because we have only been able to meet with the children once a week, so we needed to read the book and have a discussion in one, forty-five-minute class period. But chapter books are also suitable for philosophical discussions with children if one has the ability to meet with them more often or if one focuses on a single chapter, as we do with *The Wonderful Wizard of Oz* (Baum 2000).

Each of the books that we use in our course was chosen because it raises important issues in one of the above-mentioned fields of philosophy. For example, the question of what constitutes bravery is one that raises significant ethical issues, for it asks us to think about why we think that being brave is a good thing, assuming we do, and how we can tell that someone is brave. "Dragons and Giants," a story from *Frog and Toad Together* (Lobel 1999), raises these questions in a humorous and engaging manner by raising puzzles about how a person could say that he was being brave at the same time as he ran as fast as he could to evade something dangerous. As a result, I decided to use this story to introduce ethics to the school children.

Analogous things can be said about each of the other books or stories that together make up our elementary-school introduction to philosophy course. By combining them, we can acquaint the children with most of the central areas of philosophy, though we only look at one small topic or set of topics within each of them in a manner similar to most college-level introductory courses. We leave more intensive explorations of any of these areas for future sessions!

Now that you have a general idea of what our introduction to philosophy course is like, I'll describe how a typical session of elementary-school philosophy instruction proceeds. The first time we go into a class, we have a general discussion with the children about what's involved in having a philosophical discussion. We explain to them that philosophy requires them to act differently than they are used to, because they have to think very hard, listen to their classmates even harder, and figure out if they agree or disagree with what has been said. In addition, we emphasize that philosophy is not so much about saying *what* you think but *why* you think it.

To help the children remember what is required of them, we post a list entitled "How We Do Philosophy!" We try to give them a sense of philosophy as having special rules, just as I explained in the last chapter. You can see the list in table 5.2.

Table 5.2. How We Do Philosophy!

1. We *answer* the questions the teacher asks as clearly as we can.
2. We *listen* carefully and quietly to what someone is saying.
3. We *think* about what we heard.
4. We *decide* if we *agree or disagree*.
5. We think about *why* we agree or disagree.
6. When the teacher calls on us, we say whether we agree or not and why.
7. We *respect* what everyone says.
8. We *all* have valuable contributions to make.
9. We *have fun* thinking together!

For reasons that should be clear by now, we begin every session with a read-aloud. Philosophy discussions work best with groups of roughly six to twelve students—enough to have a discussion and differing opinions, but not so many that the children get frustrated because they can't express their views often enough. Sitting in a circle with the students, the facilitator begins by going over the rules we post about *how we do philosophy*. If it's our first session, she spends more time, asking the students what they think of each rule, whether it might be important, and even changing a rule if the students think that's important.

The reading of the story is always a lot of fun. I always advise my students to ham it up *more* than they want to. The stories we read are very entertaining, so we want the students to be really engaged by them. As the facilitator reads, she pauses from time to time at a well-chosen place to make sure that everyone has understood what's happened in the story. Everyone should be an active participant in our discussions, so we don't want attention problems or comprehension difficulties to stymie anyone.

Not all elementary-school children are as comfortable moving immediately from the read-aloud to an abstract discussion of a philosophical issue. In order to make sure that everyone is able to follow what we're doing, we have learned to begin our discussion of the book with a chart. We use those large pads that populate elementary-school classrooms, so that all of the children can help us fill in the chart. The chart generally begins by displaying the central elements of the story that we will be discussing, but it moves on from there, as we ask the children to fill in information, as a first, gentle step in our philosophical discussion.

When we teach *The Important Book* (Brown 1990), for example, we choose three of the objects upon which the book focuses—a spoon, an apple, and you—and list everything that the book says about them. Doing this helps get all the children in a position to discuss whether they agree with the book's assertions about what is important about each of these things. (For more on *The Important Book*, see chapter 10.)

Central to our method for discussing philosophy with children are the questions that the facilitator poses to them. We have prepared sets of questions for each of the books that will help you get at the philosophical issues that each story raises. My students, my colleagues, and I have spent a lot of time figuring out what philosophical questions are raised by each book and how best to get children to approach them.

This is not an easy undertaking. I remember working with my students as they were preparing to teach "The Dream," another story from *Frog and Toad Together* (Lobel 1999). It is a story in which Frog has a dream in which he keeps getting bigger and Toad keeps getting smaller, until Toad vanishes and Frog wakes up in a panic. We had been using the story to teach an issue in epistemology, namely, how we know that we are not now dreaming if, as the story illustrates, dreams can be so vivid that we are not sure, even once we are awake, whether they were really dreams or not. Suddenly, as my students were discussing that issue, it dawned on me that the story was really about the morality of bragging. Although I had taught the story myself and used it in my class for years, my own preconceptions had kept me from seeing that there was an ethical issue very relevant to young children—why it might not be in someone's interest to brag—that I had simply overlooked.

I mention this not to scare you but so that you will realize how much assistance the question sets can give you. For each story, we have developed a series of questions that you can use to raise what we believe are the story's most important philosophical questions in a way that will stimulate discussion. This is important because it does take some knowledge to determine what philosophical issues a story raises. By preselecting questions for you, we have attempted to ensure that you can direct your students toward philosophically significant issues raised by the story that you want them to discuss. This lets you engage them in philosophical discussions without having to decide on your own what philosophical issues a story actually raises.

I have one piece of advice whose importance I want to underscore. When I first started using these question sets, my students tended to use them as recipes:

Step 1: Ask question 1.
Wait for an answer.
Step 2: Ask question 2.
Wait for an answer. And so on.

I know that this was the result of insecurity and nervousness, but the result was that discussions were often stifled prematurely because my students were trying to keep the discussion moving instead of *listening* to what the children had to say. My students didn't realize that, in general, the best way to move the discussion forward is *not* asking a new question, but focusing on the answer a child has already given and asking the others what they think of it.

One thing that I have learned through my engagement with teaching children philosophy is how little we listen to each other. In the classroom, children generally vie with one another for their teacher's attention and pay little attention to what their classmates say. Adults hear what children say, but often fail to really listen to them, to consider what they really are saying or asking.

One of the great virtues of doing philosophy with children is that it forces you to *listen* to them. It's a skill my students have to learn, in part because their own anxieties about being in a classroom make it difficult for them to really listen to what the children are saying. But that is something they need to do.

So, it's very important not to think of the questions in the question sets as simply needing an answer. They really should function as *prompts* for discussion. This means that, when a child answers a question, your role is to get the other children to focus upon what he has said and to respond to it using one of the appropriate "moves" I detailed in the last chapter. Among other things, you are trying to get the children to see that they can really learn through their interactions with one another, something that may be a unique experience for them.

It's for this reason that I suggest that you use the question set I provide for each book as the basis for a lesson plan of your own devising. The lesson plan should be your working out of how you would like the discussion to go, at least ideally. But remember not to force the discussion to proceed as *you* want it to. It's the children's discussion, and they should be able to determine how it develops.

To make you more comfortable with facilitating discussions of philosophical topics you may not know a great deal about, in the following chapters I have also provided introductions to those issues. You don't actually *have* to read them. But I know that many teachers will feel more comfortable leading a discussion if they have some knowledge of the topic. My philosophical introductions should give you enough knowledge to feel comfortable without boring you with a great deal of detail. (There are also suggestions for further investigation in the Appendix, if you are interested in learning more about any topic.) Getting used to facilitating discussions about topics for which you don't have the answer—indeed, for which there may be no agreed upon answer—is hard. But it is also what makes it so much fun to work with children in this way: You may learn as much from them as they will from you.

In chapter 7, I give more detailed advice about how to lead a philosophical discussion. Now, I want to return to my discussion of our classroom sessions. We generally do not spend more than forty-five minutes with the children discussing the book. Having a philosophical discussion requires a lot of attention from everyone, so we don't want to wear the children out, allowing their attention to flag, a sure prelude to "classroom management" issues. But it's also important to allow enough time for the discussion to get going. In consultation with classroom teachers, we've settled on forty-five minutes as a good general limit.

This, then, in outline is what our elementary-school introduction of philosophy is like. In the balance of the book, I will, first, explain how to make a lesson plan and how to lead a philosophical discussion, two necessary components for a good session with the children. I will then present each of the eight books that make up our course. For each book, I will outline the philosophical issues it raises and then describe how you might lead a discussion that focuses on those issues, followed by the actual question set we have devised for the book. The idea is that you will use both my discussion and the question set to prepare your own lesson plan for each book.

6

PREPARING A LESSON PLAN

It's now time to get more specific. You may be wondering exactly how you should go about preparing to lead a philosophical discussion of a children's book. I will now give you some very concrete suggestions about how to get ready to do so.

The most crucial preparation you can make is developing a lesson plan like the one you can find at the end of this chapter. At least for your initial philosophical discussions, this is a critical element of your preparation, one that I require that my students always use. In addition to the sample lesson plan at the end of this chapter, I have provided a form that you can use in developing your own. Working out a lesson plan will not only prepare you to lead the discussion, but will also make you more confident that you have a clear idea of how you want the discussion to proceed.

Elementary-school children have had very different levels of acquaintance with books. In our increasingly digitized world, books no longer occupy the place they one did in our relations with our children. The consequence of this displacement is that not every child will be used to following a story that is read to her from a book. Depending on how adept your students are at understanding the read-aloud stories and on the level of the book you have chosen, you may need to take a few preparatory steps before getting to the philosophical discussion proper.

A first step you might need to take is figuring out if the book you will be teaching contains any vocabulary words that might be difficult for some of your students. If there are, you should make a list of them on your lesson plan and begin your session by discussing them with the students. You can ask if any of them know what the words mean and then get them to use the words in sentences. Doing so will help the students grasp the story you read, though you should make sure they remember the definitions when the words occur in the story.

Sometimes, it is useful to prepare students by getting them to think about the issues the story raises. One way to do this is to have them look at the cover and discuss what hints it gives them regarding the subject of the story. You could ask them about both the title and the cover illustration, seeing what expectations they might have about the story just from these two features. This is also a good way to get the students all talking, an objective you need to keep in mind as you lead the discussion. So include this step in your plan if you think it appropriate.

As you read the book aloud, you need to be sure that the children are following the events in the plot. So, in your lesson plan, you should make notes of where you might want to stop and get the children to summarize what's taken place. You might also want to have some initial discussions of certain ideas during the reading itself, though you don't want to distract the children from the story and make it harder for them to follow it.

When you finish reading the story, it's good to make sure that everyone understands what's happened. This could involve asking the students to summarize the story's plot. Or, you could ask them specific questions about what took place, aiming to make sure that they all understand exactly what transpired in the story. At this stage, you should only be trying to make sure that every child is in a position to take part in the discussion.

Another strategy you shouldn't hesitate to use is asking the children if there is anything they didn't understand or were not clear about. Again, noting in your lesson plan specific difficulties that might arise is a good way to prepare for leading this part of the discussion. This is also the time to fill out the chart that I recommend you use.

We use charts to put the information from the books—this might include elements of the plot, the attitudes of the characters, the children's assessments of what took place, and so on—into a form that enables the children to discuss the stories more easily. Although many children do not need them, the charts form an intermediary step between the read-aloud and the philosophical discussion. We have found that some children are enabled to participate in our discussions more fully because of them.

You are now ready to plan the philosophical part of your discussion. You should use the questions set you find at the end of each chapter for doing this. In reading the questions, familiarize yourself with the philosophical issues raised by the story and think about how you would feel most comfortable raising them with your students. This part of your lesson plan should be an adaptation of the question set in a way that you think would best stimulate discussion. You need to think about raising questions so that they follow one another in a logical sequence. So, please, pick and choose among the questions as you see fit, and even add ones of your own if you think they make sense and will assist you in discussing the story. Our questions are convenient guides that you should use in developing your lesson plan. There is absolutely no need to follow them slavishly. You'll do a better job if you adapt them in light of your own ideas.

In developing our question sets, we have striven to present the individual questions in a logical sequence. Generally, the idea is to begin with more specific and concrete questions, and then to move to more abstract and general ones. There are a variety of reasons for this. As I have already mentioned, it is important to try to get every student involved in the discussion. Beginning with questions that relate to their own experience, for example, can give students a way to participate, even if they are not yet ready to enter the abstract discussions completely.

As you develop your plan, focus on having questions and strategies that will allow every student to make a contribution to the discussion. In doing this, you need to be careful not to ask questions that are so abstract that the students will not know how to respond to them. So, for example, after reading "Dragons and Giants" (Lobel 1999), it's not a good idea to ask, "What is bravery?" because that question is so abstract that it's not clear to the students—or, indeed, most of us—how to answer it.

It's also very important not to ask a leading question, that is, a question whose answer you know and want the children to supply. I liken the result of asking such questions to "fishing expeditions," as each child tries to guess what you want them to say. Such attempts to satisfy the teacher are antithetical to our attempt to create a learner-centered teaching environment in the classroom and need to be studiously avoided!

Each question set generally includes questions on more than one philosophical topic. This is because the stories themselves generally raise multiple philosophical issues. You should pick and choose among these groups of questions, deciding which you feel would work best with your students.

One good technique that you should note in your plan and try to use early in the discussion is the "go-round." The go-round proceeds when you ask an easy question that each student will be able to answer. Sometimes this will involve asking them to give an example from their own experience of the phenomenon in question, but it can also be more abstract. For example, if there is an illustration in the book that is relevant to the discussion, you might ask each student to say what he or she likes or dislikes about the picture. Planning to have some go-rounds in your lesson is a good way to ensure that all the children will participate in the discussion.

Finally, use your lesson plan to remind yourself of things you need to do in the discussion, such as giving the children lots of positive feedback or listening carefully to what they say. Having that advice before you in black and white can be an important means of getting yourself to remember what you want to do in leading the discussion.

But don't treat the lesson plan as setting up a fixed direction that the discussion has to take. It's there to help you begin the discussion and keep track of the central philosophical issues raised by the story. When you actually hear the kids responding to you, you should be prepared to follow the discussion wherever it leads, so long as it remains philosophically pertinent.

The next couple of pages have two documents that will be useful to you as you begin planning to facilitate a discussion. The first is an example of a lesson plan for "Dragons and Giants" that I have developed and that will give you a sense of how to go about creating one. You can compare it to the question set at the end of chapter 8 in order to see how far one can depart from a question set in developing a good lesson plan. The second is a form that you can use for your lesson plan. I urge you to copy it and fill it out, as you prepare to lead your discussion. I hope both of these are helpful and make it easier for you to begin—and enjoy!—teaching philosophy.

SAMPLE LESSON PLAN

Lesson Plan for Philosophical Discussion of "Dragons and Giants" from *Frog and Toad Together*

Author: Arnold Lobel
Vocabulary: avalanche
Before Reading:

1. Ask if they've read Frog and Toad stories before.
2. If so, ask what is the relationship between Frog and Toad and, looking at the cover, which is which.
3. Ask what the title suggests to them, where they might have read or heard any stories about dragons and giants.

During Reading:

1. Can you see what book Frog and Toad are reading? Do you know any fairy tales? Who is brave in them?
2. Focus on the snake incident by asking them if they are afraid of snakes? What would they have done in Frog and Toad's place?
3. Remind them of what an avalanche is. Ask them why it is scary.
4. Ask them why Frog and Toad are scared of the hawk. Would they be?

After Reading:
Begin by filling out chart. (See Table 6.1)

Table 6.1. How Frog and Toad Try to Figure Out Whether They Are Brave

What Frog and Toad Do	*Are They Being Brave?*
Look in a mirror	Yes or No?
Run from the snake	Yes or No?
Run from the avalanche	Yes or No?
Run from the hawk	Yes or No?
Hide in the closet and under the covers	Yes or No?

Questions for Discussion:

1. Have you ever done anything that you think is brave? In just two or three sentences, give us an example of what you did that was brave.
2. Choose one example given by the students and ask why he or she thought it was brave. Try to get the students to come up with one or two criteria for an action being brave.
3. Do you think that running away from the snake was a brave thing to do? Why or why not?
4. Can you be afraid and still do something brave?
5. What about if a bully dared you to walk on a train track and you knew that a train might come by? Would it be brave to do what he said? Would it be brave to refuse?
6. Give an example of someone—either a real person or a fictional character—who you think is brave. Explain why you think he or she is brave.

LESSON PLAN FORM

(Feel free to copy)

Lesson Plan for Philosophical Discussion of ________________

Author:

Vocabulary: (3–5 words)

Before Reading:

1.

2.

3.

4.

5.

During Reading:

1.

2.

3.

4.

5.

Questions for Discussion:

1.

2.

3.

4.

5.

7

LEADING A PHILOSOPHICAL DISCUSSION

In earlier chapters, I explained how it is possible for someone without a great deal of specialized philosophical knowledge to lead a philosophical discussion among elementary-school children. The crucial thing to remember is that the teacher serves as both the initiator and regulator of a philosophical discussion but not as a dispenser of philosophical knowledge to the children. As a result, although it will be helpful for the teacher to know what constitutes a good philosophical discussion, she does not need to have a great deal of specialized knowledge about the topics that will be discussed. Indeed, even though teachers don't usually possess this "expert" knowledge, they can still be very effective in leading philosophical discussions in their classrooms.

Nonetheless, leading a philosophical discussion with children can be intimidating, especially the first time. Partly, this is because we are not used to thinking of education as what I have called a "learner-centered" process. Most of the time, we revert to older ways of thinking according to which teachers are knowledgeable and students are ignorant. It's certainly very comfortable to be in the position of the knowledgeable one. You then know what you've got to do: Transmit the knowledge that you have to your charges who lack it. But it's a very different story when you are leading a discussion of a subject about which you don't have much more knowledge than your students and where you are asking open-ended questions for which you don't know the answers! How can you feel comfortable with this unusual role?

I've already presented one piece of advice about providing yourself with something that will help you be effective in your new role as facilitator: having a lesson plan. The lesson plan provides you with a certain amount of security, for it has a series of questions that you can ask the students. I know that it's scary to try to lead an open-ended discussion, because you just can't be sure of where it might go. When I first started teaching, I was petrified of class discussions because I didn't think I would be able to direct them effectively. It took me a long time to develop the self-confidence necessary to allow students more freedom in the classroom. But once I did, I realized that leading a discussion wasn't so hard, for the students were eager to have a meaningful discussion of the issues we were talking about.

Elementary-school children are no different. With your assistance, they will take to the game of philosophy readily. If you are prepared with your lesson plan, you can help your students explore a range of fascinating issues. And who knows? You might even learn from their comments!

To assist you in your efforts, I've also provided introductions to the philosophical issues raised by each story. These are intended to give you overviews of what philosophical questions are raised by the stories and outlines of what philosophers think about them. One of the important features of philosophy is that virtually none of the issues lying at its core has received a definitive resolution in the two and a half millennia that they have been discussed. This means that, rather than having widely accepted answers, these questions have two or more competing proposed solutions whose viability philosophers continue to discuss and debate. For each issue raised by a story, my philosophical introductions acquaint you with some of these competing positions. My hope is that, by having a general sense of what views philosophers have put forward in an attempt to answer these questions, you will be better able to recognize and encourage the philosophically astute responses that your students will make.

I have already discussed the question sets. So let me just remind you that my students and I have thought long and hard about how best to begin a philosophical discussion for each book. The result is the question set, a series of questions about each book that can guide you in initiating and continuing a philosophical discussion among your students. In this way, you don't need to decide by yourself what the central issues raised by a book are, but can rely on our having already done so. Your own lesson plan will have used our questions as suggestions that you have adapted to your students' skills, abilities, and interests.

I now want to present the advice that I give my own students for leading a philosophical discussion. Much of this will be old hat to experienced teachers. But I include it all here for the benefit of anyone interested in having philosophical discussions with children who might profit from it.

There are six pieces of advice for leading a successful philosophical discussion among elementary-school children that I always emphasize to my students (summarized in table 7.1):

1. *Be prepared!* Although this is the most obvious piece of advice I can give you, it is still incredibly important. You need to acquaint yourself thoroughly with the book you will be teaching the students. Of course, this requires that you have read the book at least a couple of times. It probably would be good to make at least one of those readings a read-aloud, so you can see how the story sounds and if there are any tricky passages that need a bit of work. You can also practice "hamming it up," say, by developing different voices for each of the characters, if you are up to the challenge.

   It's also important, as I emphasized in the last chapter, to go over the question set and create a lesson plan in which you put the ones you think are the most important, the ones you really want to ask. Finally, you may find it helpful to have a basic understanding of how philosophers have thought about the philosophical issues raised by the story, so that you can recognize a good response and call the kids' attention to it. My introductions are intended to help you with this.
2. *Show excitement!* Your success will depend a lot on how the kids perceive you. Show them that you are very interested in them and are excited to be teaching them. This shouldn't be hard, but remember not to let any anxiety you might have about teaching

philosophy get in the way of showing them that you really are having a great time talking to them.

3. *LISTEN!* In my experience, this is hard, especially at first. You probably will be nervous and you have a plan full of questions in your head. The temptation is to ask a question and then, after a kid responds, to just ask the next one, your hands shaking.

   Don't do it! You need to listen to what they are saying and try to get them to respond to what their classmate has said. If no one else has a hand raised to respond, ask an improvised follow-up question to keep the discussion moving and focused on the issue that has been raised.

   Our central concern is to have the children fully discuss each issue that you bring up. There is absolutely no pressure on you to "get through" all the questions in a given question set or lesson plan. In fact, the danger of having a lesson plan is that it can seem as if you need to do what it says. Remember that it is just a general guide that gives you a sense of the lay of the philosophical land. Don't let it get in the way of paying attention to the children's own claims.

   So if you ask a question and a good philosophical discussion develops, that's great! Stick with it. Remember, your only goal is to provide an opportunity for the children to have a philosophical conversation with one another on a particular topic. Don't worry at all about "coverage." There's no harm in leaving some issues raised by a book unexplored. You can always decide to return to them during a future philosophy session.

4. *Give your students "markers."* Markers are comments that indicate that they've accomplished something during their discussion. If you've had a discussion of some topic, don't just move on to the next question. You need to *mark* how the discussion has progressed so that the students can recognize what they have accomplished. One of the real dangers of engaging elementary-school students in philosophical discussions is that, because there are no definitive answers to be had, they will feel that the discussion went nowhere and be very frustrated. Children themselves are quick to conform to the expectations that we have for them. Like you, they are not used to having philosophical discussions at school. It's very

important that you show them that they can learn something even though no definitive answer has emerged.

For example, even though no consensus may have been reached, progress is made when a question is clarified or new alternatives are proposed. It's crucial therefore that you, as a facilitator, get the students to recognize what they have accomplished during their discussion. This is the point of giving them clear markers—as well as frequent praise for their efforts.

I want to emphasize that progress in a philosophical discussion can take place in many ways. Even having a disagreement can count as progress when the alternatives are posed more clearly than they were prior to the discussion. In such cases, you might say something like, "We've had a really interesting discussion of what makes an action fair. I think we have a real disagreement here. Some of you think that only things that help everyone are fair, while others disagree. That's really interesting because . . . Maybe we should move on to another question now."

Also, remember to be lavish in your praise of the children when they have had a good discussion of an issue. Telling a student that he has made a good comment is a great way to stimulate further discussion as well as to provide the class with a marker of their progress.

5. *Remember to be a facilitator and not a participant in the discussion!* Your goal is to get the kids to talk with one another about the issues, not tell them what you think or what they should think. I've already discussed a variety of techniques you can use to keep them talking to each other, such as asking, "What do the rest of you think about what Latifa just said?" Or, "Does anyone disagree with Colin, that bravery is really stupid?" Or, "Let's go around the circle and each of you share an example of something brave that you have done."
6. *Enjoy yourself!* If you are not too nervous and are able to focus on what the kids say, leading a philosophical discussion can be a really fun and rewarding experience. I always learn something from doing philosophy with children. Remember, they are natural-born philosophers, so we can all learn from them. And they are funny and cute, as well as intelligent. So give yourself over to the experience and enjoy it!

Table 7.1. The Six Pieces of Advice for Facilitators

1. Be prepared!
2. Show excitement!
3. Listen to what the children say!
4. Give markers!
5. Remember to be a facilitator and not a participant in the discussion!
6. Enjoy yourself!

THE STORIES

8

"DRAGONS AND GIANTS": TEACHING ETHICS

Ethics forms a very important part of the discipline of philosophy. The basic focus of ethics is on how we humans ought to live our lives. In exploring this issue, ethics has to distinguish the more worthwhile paths we can tread from less valued ones. There are people each of us admires for how they conduct themselves and we generally would use some term of praise to register this admiration, say, by calling them good, virtuous, or admirable. Similarly, there are people whose lives we can all point to as prime examples of how not to live; indeed, the truly evil people in the world may stand out in a way that the good ones often do not. Ethics investigates the rationality of the practice of making such value judgments about the conduct of our lives.

Aristotle (384–322 BCE), one of the first philosophers to clearly see the importance of arriving at a systematic account of why certain life paths are better than others, suggested that we should think of *virtues* as character states that human beings ought to have. He based his claim on the recognition that there are certain very basic types of situations that human beings are likely to encounter in the course of their lives. For example, every human being will likely experience situations that they judge to be dangerous, that is, situations in which they find themselves confronted by something scary that makes them afraid. Similarly, there are many times when we find ourselves wanting something that may or may not be good for us. Aristotle's idea was that there is a specific virtue—such as bravery or moderation—that can guide individuals in the appropriate situations in making appropriate decisions and performing appropriate actions (Aristotle 1999).

To see how this works, imagine that I live in a mountainous area where the trails I walk on have frequent, rather large ravines over which I have to jump to get to where I want to go. (Let's assume that the ravines are big and very scary because they go way, way down.) What's the best way to handle such situations?

One answer would be to engage in tough physical training, so that I would never blanch in the face of any danger so paltry as a simple ravine. But I think most of us would think this not the best thing to do, for there could be ravines so vast that it would be a mistake for me to blithely assume that I could jump even one of them. Far better, I think, for me to develop more than one capacity: I need to have the self-confidence necessary for jumping ravines that are reasonable to jump but also the ability to judge which ravines I can jump and which ones I can't, so that I would know when to jump and when not to.

How can we describe this situation philosophically? One possibility is to say that bravery, which is the capacity to deal appropriately with dangerous situations, has more than one component. First, it involves *self-confidence*, meaning not just the feeling that I can do certain things, but the experience on which to base it. Second, it involves *judgment*, or knowing which dangerous situations are ones that I am likely to be able to deal with successfully and which not, as well an understanding of when it might be worth facing a danger one knows one may not conquer.

On this analysis, bravery is composed of two basic capacities, judgment and self-confidence. For someone to be brave, she must have each of these in just the right proportion. A person who lacks judgment and whose self-confidence appears infinite is *rash*, for she will face dangers she would do well to avoid. On the other hand, a person with sound judgment but no self-confidence will be overwhelmed by every danger she faces. Realizing that dangers by nature pose some sort of threat to herself, such a person will be incapacitated and unable therefore to face the dangers. She will be *cowardly*, the contrary moral failing to being rash.

I have just presented an analysis of bravery as an Aristotelian "virtue," that is, a state of a person's character that is well suited to dealing with a specific type of situation that human beings can be expected to face during their lives. The situation for which bravery is appropriate is one in which a person is faced with a danger that must be met with the right balance of self-confidence and judgment. This virtue has two "vices," or defects, that are caused by a preponderance of one of the components (self-confidence or judgment) over the other—rashness and cowardice.

The basic idea of this *virtue theory* of ethics, then, is that an ethical or good person is one who cultivates the virtues, for this will allow her to deal appropriately with the typical situations that human beings are likely to face in the course of their lives. Such a person will be able to surmount dangers, avoid temptation, not overindulge their appetites, and so forth.

Aristotle's theory of the virtues has been so influential that much of our commonsense understanding of ethical behavior reflects it, though we are generally not conscious of this. Our goal in this session with the children is to get them to think about their own understanding of what makes a person brave.

Arnold Lobel's story "Dragons and Giants" from *Frog and Toad Together* (1999) works really well for this purpose. Lobel wrote a series of stories about two amphibians, Frog and Toad, who are good friends and who often succumb to puzzlement, a state of being that is characteristic of philosophers. In this particular story, Frog and Toad puzzle over what makes someone brave. After looking in a mirror to see if they are as brave as the characters they have been reading about in fairy tales, they go on a walk to discover if they are brave. During their walk, they encounter many scary things that give them ample opportunity to test their bravery. Frog and Toad's responses to the dangers they face provide the fuel for an elementary-school discussion of bravery, for the children will be genuinely puzzled about whether Frog and Toad have responded to the different things that threaten them as bravely as they explicitly say they have.

A good place to start your discussion of bravery is by making a chart (see table 8.1). Begin by asking the children to tell you all of the things that Frog and Toad do to see if they are brave. You should list their responses on the chart. Then, for each of those actions, ask the children

Table 8.1. How Frog and Toad Try to Figure Out Whether They Are Brave

What Frog and Toad Do	*Are They Being Brave?*
Look in a mirror	??
Run from the snake	??
Run from the avalanche	??
Run from the hawk	??
Hide in the closet and under the covers	??

?? indicates that children may have different views.

(1) whether Frog and Toad said they were brave when they did them and (2) whether the children think they were actually brave.

The discussion can then take off from the first entry in the chart: Frog and Toad looking at themselves in a mirror to see if they are brave. (Make sure the children notice the book entitled *Fairy Tales* that Toad holds in his hands.) This raises the question of whether you can look at someone and tell whether she is brave. You can ask the children whether they have a "brave" look. Some of them might and others might not. You could then follow up by asking what it is about those brave looks that shows that they are brave. This allows you to get a sense of what their initial, unreflective notion of bravery is. If one of them says that bravery can't be seen, that it's *something inside*, you have an opening for further discussion.

As you continue this discussion, you might ask if there are certain types of people who are brave. Here, one can imagine firemen, cowboys, soldiers, and the like being cited. Again, once the children have put forward some examples of brave people, it's important to ask them why they think those people are brave, for they will presumably say something about the *dangers* they face.

By looking at the initial moves suggested for a discussion of "Dragons and Giants," you can see an important feature of a philosophical discussion that distinguishes it from other types of discussions that we frequently have with children. First, we begin with an idea that comes from the story—Is there a way to look brave?—and we immediately move up a level of abstraction by **asking** what about such a look makes it a brave one. This is significant, for one of the characteristics of philosophy is its *generality*, and we can see here how this comes about: We start with a basic level phenomenon and **jump** up a level with a well-posed question that gets the children to reflect about the same subject (here, bravery) in a more abstract and general manner.

As the discussion proceeds, you need to pay very careful attention to what the children have said. Although there is a logic to the development of the story that we might ideally wish the children to follow, as a facilitator, you need to listen with open and highly attuned ears to what the children are saying so that you can help them make the move toward abstraction that is characteristic of philosophy in a way that is appropriate to their own discussion, not to your intentions. The discussion belongs to them; you are only its facilitator.

This means that, as you pay careful attention to what the children are saying, you may have to follow their lead rather than take the discussion in the direction that you anticipated. Although we are aiming to encourage a philosophical discussion among the children, we want them to have control over the direction the discussion takes.

At this point, there are many ways that the discussion could proceed. You could ask the children whether a person who faces each and every danger that comes her way really is a brave person. If they seem to think she is, you can ask them to engage in what philosophers call a "thought experiment."

Thought experiments are imaginary scenarios that philosophers devise to get us to see their point of view. So you can ask the children to imagine that a huge monster has come to town. Would the person who walks up to the monster and says, "Go away! You are frightening everyone!" really be brave? The idea would be to get them to discuss the idea that a brave person has the self-confidence to face danger, but he also has to have the judgment to know when doing so would be rash. Taking on a vicious monster that is bigger and stronger than you would be rash rather than brave.

Reflecting on the roles on self-confidence and judgment in bravery has not moved the discussion to a more abstract level; instead, it has developed a more sophisticated understanding of the components of bravery, focusing on self-confidence and judgment as the two elements that go to make up bravery itself. This development points to an additional characteristic of a philosophical discussion: an idea is initially put forward but then is seen to require development by reflection on whether it is adequate to understanding the phenomenon in question.

Here, we are encouraging the children to think more carefully about bravery in the expectation that they will notice that it has two components, self-confidence and judgment. Of course, they will not express themselves using such sophisticated vocabulary. They are more likely to say, "That wasn't brave. It was stupid!" But when they do so, they are registering the type of distinction we have been conceptualizing in these more complex terms.

Let me add two warnings here. First, you need to have faith that the discussion will develop along philosophically interesting lines. You can help make this happen by recognizing when a child has made a philosophically relevant suggestion and marking it with a comment like, "That was a really interesting point you just made, Mathilda! Who agrees with what Mathilda said and tell me why?"

But you also have to be prepared for how the children might respond to a question like "What's something that you have done that you consider to be brave?" You need to be aware that many of the children you are encouraging to discuss philosophy may come from social backgrounds that are different than yours and that this might affect how they respond to questions. This means that you need to be ready for almost anything.

What would you have done if one of the young and very cute second graders you were teaching responded to your question about doing something brave by saying, "A grown-up hit me in the face with a glass bottle and I was brave when I didn't cry and took all the pieces of glass out of my face by myself"? The college student who told me that one of the children she was teaching responded this way said that she was overwhelmed and thought, "Who am I to teach this child anything about bravery?"

That's precisely the sort of response you need to avoid, though hopefully you won't all get faced with such difficult situations very often. This unfortunate young boy had actually said two things about bravery that could have been the subject for a conversation with his peers: He thought that crying would have meant that he was not brave and also that he could not ask someone for help and still be brave. My student should have taken control of herself—a virtue that, incidentally, forms the subject matter of another Frog and Toad story, "Cookies" (Lobel 1999)—and asked an appropriate question that would have allowed that boy's response to initiate a philosophical discussion, such as "Why do you think that not crying and taking the glass pieces out of your face all on your own was brave?"

By the way, I have been astounded by what people are willing to reveal about themselves when they are discussing "Dragons and Giants." One of the first workshops I did at the Jackson Street Elementary School was for a number of the teachers there. We read "Dragons and Giants," and I asked them if there was something that they had done that they thought was brave.

In response, one teacher talked about dealing with her breast cancer. She felt that the way she had dealt with that was the bravest thing she had ever done. Another talked about raising a son with a mental disability. She said that it took great bravery to keep on doing all that she needed to do. Each teacher revealed a facet of their lives that was not visible to me but showed that they were acting with great courage in facing real difficulties. And the session may have helped them by getting them to see themselves as living real profiles in courage.

The question set that follows provides you with various questions that you can use to continue your discussion with the children. It includes a variety of questions about the nature of bravery, such as whether a brave person can actually be scared. My experience is that children have a lot to say about the issues concerning bravery raised by "Dragons and Giants."

I have said that there are many benefits to be had from introducing philosophy into elementary-school classrooms. One that I have not yet emphasized is that it can help children think about stresses in their own lives differently. "Dragons and Giants" is a good example of a story that can have this effect. One problem that elementary-school children often worry about is bullying. Bullies generally try to get kids to do dangerous things the children know they shouldn't by daring them to do something on pain of being "chicken." Reflecting on "Dragons and Giants" and the idea that it can be stupid to do something really dangerous can help children understand their own situation very differently than they previously had, to see that refusing to do what a bully demands might actually be braver than giving in to the pressure to do what they have dared them to. But if they can come to see things this way as a result of discussing "Dragons and Giants," it's because they have learned something through their communal investigation of bravery, rather than from us imposing our views on them.

"DRAGONS AND GIANTS" FROM *FROG AND TOAD TOGETHER*, BY ARNOLD LOBEL

Questions for Philosophical Discussion

Topic: Looking Brave *Frog and Toad look in a mirror to see if they are brave. Frog says they look brave. Toad asks if they really are brave.*

1. How do you look when you are being brave?
2. Can you tell by looking at someone whether they are brave or not?
3. Was there ever a time when you felt brave but didn't look brave?
4. Can you look frightened but still be brave?
5. How could Frog and Toad tell that they were looking brave?

Topic: Bravery and Danger *Frog says that trying to climb a mountain should tell him and Toad whether they are brave.*

1. Does doing something that is hard to do show that you are brave?
2. Are there other ways to show that you are brave?
3. Does doing something that's dangerous show that you are brave?
4. What if someone makes you do it?
5. What if you do something dangerous but don't know it's dangerous? Can you still be brave?

Topic: Perceiving Bravery *Frog and Toad wonder whether they are brave.*

1. How do you know when you're being brave?
2. If someone says that you are brave, does this mean that you are?
3. How can other people tell when you are being brave?
4. Is it possible that you might think you are brave and be wrong?
5. Can other people be wrong if they think that you are not brave?

Topic: Bravery and Fear *When the snake tries to eat Frog and Toad, they jump away and Toad starts shaking.*

1. Were Frog and Toad being brave even though they jumped away?
2. What else could they have done?
3. Is it ever brave to run away from something dangerous?
4. Was Toad brave even though he was shaking with fear?
5. Does being scared when you face danger show that you aren't really brave?
6. Is it possible to be brave and afraid at the same time?

Topic: Bravery and Action *When Frog and Toad get back to Toad's house, Toad jumps into bed and pulls the cover up over his head. Frog jumps into the closet and shuts the door.*

1. Does hiding under the covers or in the closet show that you are not brave?
2. Does a brave person have to be brave all of the time?
3. Can you run away from something scary and still be brave?

9

FREDERICK: TEACHING SOCIAL AND POLITICAL PHILOSOPHY

The fundamental question of social and political philosophy is what types of social and political arrangements are legitimate. For example, most societies accept the existence of both social and economic differences among the individuals who make them up. In such societies, some people are wealthier than others, and prestige is also distributed unequally. At the same time, a democratic society is founded, at least in theory, on the notion of "one person, one vote," that is, in this respect, democracies do not permit unequal distribution of power in the political realm. One basic question that a social and political philosopher has to face, then, is, Why do we think that certain kinds of inequality are fine while we object to others?

One reason that has been offered to explain why inequality might be justifiable in the economic realm is that it is the most *expedient* way to structure society. That is, social and political philosophers argue that allowing economic inequality will promote a higher level of economic productivity (or "general welfare" in philosophers' jargon) than a system of complete economic equality. This is the idea behind so-called trickle-down economics: If you let the wealthy have benefits, the increase in productivity that results will eventually improve the lives of everyone. But even if you find this application of the idea implausible, the general idea of allowing inequality in order to provide for a higher level of overall well-being is one that many people accept.

Alternatively, some philosophers believe that equality is such an important norm or value that there is no justification for departing from it. From such a point of view, everyone should share equally in the economic benefits that society has to offer, and there is no justification for letting anyone have more than anyone else. This is the basic idea behind socialism, although it also has roots in religious traditions such as Christianity.

Many philosophers think that there needs to be some middle ground between pure expediency and absolute equality. These philosophers would allow for differences in wealth but put limits on how large such differences can be. In *A Theory of Justice* (1971), John Rawls put forward an influential principle intended to limit the extent of inequalities: *only those differences in wealth that benefit the least well-off members of society are justified*. The idea is that only those departures from equality that benefit the worst off are allowed. This view accepts the socialist claim that equality is a crucial value but tempers it with the recognition that it can be legitimate to depart from it so long as everyone benefits from so doing. It seems difficult to advocate that equality should be maintained even if everyone would be better off from allowing certain limited inequalities.

But if it is widely acknowledged that inequality in the economic sphere makes sense, why is the political sphere different? After all, we don't think anyone should get an extra vote, no matter what. Why is the assumption of equality held to be politically inviolable when it is not economically?

This differential application of the norm of equality in regard to the political and economic spheres is a very interesting topic to reflect upon. Here, I can only point to one line of argument in favor of political equality, namely, that it best ensures the legitimacy of government. Roughly, the idea is that people will be more committed to the existence of a government when they believe their share of control is equal to that which everyone else has. Allowing certain people a greater degree of control over the government would cause people not to feel allegiance to it.

One aspect of philosophy that social and political philosophy makes clear to us is that philosophy deals with idealized situations. In American society, there is no question that, despite the "one person, one vote" principle, some people have a much greater degree of influence over government than others. This is particularly true of large corporations and very wealthy people. Their economic resources allow them to buy political influence, something most of us cannot do. But such departures from the ideal are not usually taken to be the appropriate subject for philosophical discussions of what makes certain social arrangements legitimate.

So far, I have discussed economic and political questions. What exactly makes an issue reside in the realm of *social* philosophy? Well, one pertinent example is that of gay marriage. Leaving aside a religious perspective, marriage is a legal arrangement that creates both obligations and benefits for each of the partners. The question of gay marriage, from a social point of view, is whether there are good reasons to allow heterosexual couples to have access to social benefits and obligations that nonheterosexual couples do not. Although this is a legal question, it also has broader implications, for, even if one thought there were reasons why gay couples should not be allowed to marry, there is the broader social question of whether there should be such a great inequality in social benefits—visitation rights to sick partners, being just one specific example—based upon one's sexual orientation and partner choice.

As you can see, our society has a general presumption in favor of equality, although it is one that can be overridden by other factors. A central task of social and political philosophy is to explain exactly when and to what extent such deviations should be allowed, as well as to provide some justification for the original assumption that equality is an important value.

Leo Lionni's book *Frederick* (1967) raises some of these questions in a charming and unusual manner. *Frederick* is the story of its eponymous mouse-poet. While all the other mice in Frederick's family are busy storing up various necessities for the winter, Frederick seems to be just lying around enjoying himself. When questioned by the other mice, he tells them that he is gathering colors and words for winter, responses that don't seem to satisfy them. However, during the winter, when all their supplies have run out, the mice turn to Frederick and he is able to share with them the results of all he gathered during the fall. He recites one poem that allows them to experience the colors of summer and another that explains the seasons in a mousy sort of way. By the end, the other mice realize that Frederick is a poet who provides something unique for them during the long, austere months of winter.

The central issue that *Frederick* raises is whether there is reason to think that everyone has to contribute equally to their community and what exactly counts as an equal contribution. While students will generally agree that everyone ought to make an equal contribution to their community—and here they may be thinking of the school, their family, or even their classroom—there will generally be some disagreement about whether Frederick is making an equal contribution by reciting poetry.

Early on in your discussion, it is important to be sure that the children understand what Frederick's activities of "gathering words" and "gathering sun rays" really amount to. In the book, it is clear that both are aspects of the activity of writing poems, but it is important to be sure the children understand this. It also might be useful to concentrate a little on Frederick's poems and ask the children if they like them and why.

One way to accomplish this is to make a chart that compares what Frederick does in the fall with what all the other mice do (see table 9.1). This will help the children begin to focus on the philosophical issues that are central to the story.

Once you have done this, you will want to see whether the children all agree on the importance of writing poetry. You can ask the children why they think writing poems is not as important a contribution to a group as

Table 9.1. A Comparison of What Frederick Does with What the Other Mice Do

	What the Other Mice Do	*What Frederick Does*
Activity	Gather grain, etc.	Gather colors, etc.
Why do they do it?	To survive the winter	??
Is this necessary?	Yes	??
Is this work?	Yes	??

?? indicates that children may have different views.

gathering nuts and berries, assuming that this is what they think. Generally, at least one of them will respond that writing poems is not really work. This can then lead into a discussion of what makes an activity count as work. Here, it is useful to get the children to think about their own lives and the activities they like. You might ask them whether they think that doing their homework is really work.

The question of when and why an activity should count as *work* is an extremely interesting and complex one. At first, students will be inclined to say that an activity only counts as work if it is not something you enjoy or that's fun. So they might contrast playing a game (not work) with doing manual labor (work). This would be one way to justify the idea that Frederick is not really working, for he is not doing the manual labor of gathering food that all the other mice have to engage in to prepare for the winter.

It's easy to see that this distinction won't do as it stands. You can ask the children to consider their favorite baseball player. He's doing something that's fun—playing a game—but he gets paid millions of dollars for doing it. He's working when he plays baseball, but he's taking part in an activity that's fun. (Incidentally, this example can cut either way, for a student could reply that baseball players should not be paid for doing what they do. That's actually an interesting line of thought you could follow up on.)

A more sophisticated way to justify the intuition that Frederick is not doing his part for his family/community relies on the idea that an activity counts as work only if it is something that is necessary for the continuation of the group. On this view, gathering nuts is work because it is the type of activity that needs to be done in order to keep everyone alive through the winter. The question that then arises is whether a community needs to have a poet.

In order to have a fruitful discussion at this point, it is helpful to generalize from poetry to cultural activity in general. That is, children will probably be inclined to say that poetry is not necessary for the existence of a community, but they will be less likely to say that movies, music, and television are equally superfluous.

This is where it might be helpful to try the "suitcase activity" that was developed by one of my students, Ariel Sykes. The point of this activity is to get the children to think about what they think the necessities of life are, so that people should be credited with doing something socially necessary only when they contribute to them.

To get the children to engage in the suitcase activity, read them something like the following:

> Now it is your turn to create your own suitcase for the winter. Think of four things that you would bring to survive the winter that resemble the field mice's supplies, and one or two things like Frederick's. Draw pictures that represent what you think are the most important things you will need to survive a long winter. Make sure to be very thoughtful and careful in your selection, because you will have to explain why you picked each item.

The idea behind this exercise is to provide a specific challenge to the students to think about what they really need in order to survive. It is intended to stimulate their own thinking about why it might make sense to see poetry as one of a range of activities that they themselves view as part of the necessities of life. This is not to say that this is the position they have to endorse, for one could coherently maintain that such activities are still different in kind from the activities absolutely necessary for the continuation of the community. Our aim, once again, is to get the children to think about this issue, not to take one side or the other. Having them perform this activity not only engages them in thinking through the story; it asks them to apply the ideas to their own lives.

FREDERICK, BY LEO LIONNI

Questions for Philosophical Discussion

Topic: The Nature of Community *Frederick explains that he is gathering words to use for the winter when they will run out of words.*

1. Tell us about one community that you belong to.
2. What makes that community a community?
3. Do you think that being a member of a community means that you have to contribute to it?

4. How do the mice contribute to their community? How do you contribute to yours?
5. What about Frederick? Does he contribute to the mouse community?

Topic: The Nature of Work *Frederick claims that what he does—gathering sunrays—is work.*

1. Do you think Frederick is working when he gathers the sunrays?
2. Does working have a particular feel to it?
3. If you like doing something, is it still work?
4. Does work have to be hard? Why or why not?
5. Give an example of something you do that you think is work and something you think is play. What makes one work and the other play?
6. Who is your favorite athlete? If he or she gets paid to play his or her sport, is he or she working?
7. What is your favorite subject at school? What is your least favorite subject? Is doing homework for either of them work? Why?
8. Do only adults work?
9. Is thinking work?

Topic: The Value of Poetry *At the end, all the mice realize that Frederick is a poet.*

1. Do you like Frederick's poem? Why or why not?
2. Why do people write poetry?
3. Is being a poet a job? Why or why not?
4. Do people need poetry? Is it important? Why or why not?
5. What about TV? Music?
6. If you think it is important for people to have art such as paintings, poetry, and music, can you say why?

10

THE IMPORTANT BOOK: TEACHING METAPHYSICS

Unlike some of the other fields of philosophy, metaphysics is one whose subject can initially be hard to grasp, for the central concern of metaphysics is to explicate the structure of what is or exists. This is a very abstract enterprise, so it may be difficult to get a handle on what exactly characterizes an investigation as metaphysical. The traditional understanding of metaphysics as an investigation into the nature of *being* only muddies the already murky waters.

To get a handle on the nature of metaphysics as a philosophical discipline, let's begin by thinking about all the different individual things that exist. Once you focus on some of them (think, for example, of tables and chairs) it will become apparent that these things fall into different types or classes (furniture in this case). Virtually everything that exists is a member of some class or other. So, you and I are not just individuals but instances of the general type of thing called a *human being*. Similarly, the maple tree outside of my window and the birch across the street are both trees and not merely the individual existing things, though they are that as well. In general, things fall into various basic classes that are called "species."

But that's not all the structure that reality has, for these species also fall under more general classes. Trees and flowers are both instances of the more general class of plant, just as human beings and dogs are both instances of the general class animal. And such general classes can themselves be grouped into the overarching classes of animate objects and inanimate ones, with the latter including things such as rocks and dirt. Finally, we can ascend to the most basic class of all, that of being an entity. After all, both inanimate and animate objects share something, for everything is also a *being* or an *entity*.

But now we are at the point where genuine metaphysical inquiry begins, for we can ask, What it is that makes something an entity? This is a very difficult question to wrap one's mind around. A useful piece of philosophical advice is to begin thinking about such abstract questions by comparing the concept at issue (here, entity) with its opposite (existing things that are not entities). But this may seem to be of little help, for it's not at all clear what sort of a thing a nonentity could be.

One of the most fundamental metaphysical distinctions is that between a *substance* (what I've been calling "an entity") and its *properties* or *qualities* ("things" that are not entities). Grass is an example of a substance and its color—normally green—is one of its properties. Similarly, a dog is a substance and having four legs one of its properties. If you consider any individual thing, you will see that it is a substance that has a variety of different properties. In fact, this philosophical distinction is so lodged in our commonsense approach to the world that, once it has been made, it seems so obvious that we can't remember why it was ever difficult to understand.

But now think about why we call some things substances but take others to be properties rather than substances. That is, why is *grass* a substance but its *green color* merely a property of the grass? One answer that metaphysicians have proposed is that substances can *exist independently* of other things but properties cannot. The idea is that grass is the sort of entity or being that can exist independently of other things but that its greenness must exist or reside in the grass. So the distinction between a substance and its properties is one between independent and dependent existents.

You might immediately question the validity of this distinction. After all, grass, in order to exist, needs water and minerals, at a minimum. It's not really an independent existence in any obvious sense, you might say.

With this, the philosophical discussion of the validity of the distinction between substances and their properties begins.

Faced with such problems, philosophers have proposed other grounds for making the substance-property distinction. Consider grass again. Philosophers have argued that the substance grass can exist without it having the property of being green, as it does during a draught, when it turns brown. But the grass' greenness, it is contended, is not something that can exist without being embodied in the grass. This is a second way that the distinction between independent and dependent existence has been explicated.

Let's think a bit more carefully about the relationship between one type of substance and at least some of its properties. We'll focus on the case of artifacts, things that human beings create for some purpose. A chair is an example of an artifact, for it was created for us to sit on. But now we can wonder whether something can still be a chair even if we can't sit on it. Although the answer I'm about to give can be debated, I think it reasonable to say that, if we cannot sit on something, it is not a real functioning chair. It could be, say, something that was created to be a chair but is now broken. But nothing that we cannot sit on can be a real, functioning chair.

If this idea holds in general, then, at least for one class of substances—artifacts—there is at least one property that cannot be detached from a substance without changing its nature. Philosophers have called this type of property an *essential property*, meaning that it makes up the *essence* of the thing in question, "what-it-is-to-be" that very thing and not something else. So being a chair is just being a "for-sitting-thing," so that, when an object is not one that we can sit on, it cannot be, or no longer is, a chair.

There are many other metaphysical questions besides whether the substance-property distinction has validity. For example, philosophers worry about what types of things really exist. Numbers are one example of a type of entity that some philosophers—those called "nominalists"—think do not really exist. One reason for this view is that we never encounter pure numbers in our experience but only objects that we can characterize numerically.

Without going any further a field, we are now ready to approach our elementary-school metaphysics text, *The Important Book* (Brown 1990).

This book is quite simple in structure. On each of its ten double pages, it describes one type of thing. The things discussed are a spoon, a daisy, rain, grass, snow, an apple, wind, the sky, a shoe, and, finally, you. For each of these things, some property is claimed to be "the important thing" about that item. So, for example, when discussing a spoon, the book claims that "you eat with it" is the important thing about it. A number of other properties of each object are also listed. So, the book says that a spoon is not flat but is hollow. Finally, the initial claim about the object's important property is reiterated: "But the important thing about a spoon is that you eat with it" (Brown 1990, 5).

With just a little thought, you can see that the book is making claims about what the essential property of each of the substances it considers is. For a spoon, its essential property is claimed to be the fact that one eats with it. And similar claims are made for each of the things it discusses, up to and including "you." The book thus provides a good chance for children to think about the nature of things and whether they have essential properties or not.

One of the most interesting aspects of *The Important Book* is that it makes claims about the important thing about various entities that are quite apparently *false*. For example, it says that the important thing about an apple is that it is round. There are two problems with this claim: First, apples are not really round, if what that means is circular, although it is true that they do not have points, another possible way to understand the roundness of an apple. Second, it seems perfectly possible for there to be square apples. There is nothing about what an apple is that requires it to be round.

Normally, one would not want to teach from a book that makes obvious errors such as that which *The Important Book* makes about apples. Here, however, it provides us with a great opportunity: We can use the errors in the book to teach the children the need to think for themselves and not to accept something just because they find it written in a book. This is one of the central lessons that studying philosophy teaches, and this book provides a great way of getting the children to learn it.

We suggest that you begin your lesson by concentrating on a few of the different "things" that the book discusses and putting them onto a chart. It would be best if you choose objects from different categories, such as a spoon, an apple, snow, and you. For each item, ask the kids what the book says the important thing about it is and what it says the other things that are also true about it are (see table 10.1).

Once you have made the chart, go back to the first object—a spoon in my list—and ask the children if they agree that the important thing about a spoon is that you can eat with it. You can also ask them whether, if you couldn't eat with it, it would no longer be a spoon. Then ask them about all the other things that the book says that a spoon also is. Since none of these is presented as the important thing about a spoon, something could still be a spoon and not be one of them, according to the book. This provides an opportunity to ask, for example, whether something could be a spoon even if it were flat.

At no point in the discussion do the children have to agree that the book is wrong about the essential or other properties of any object, but they will generally come to see that they don't agree with the book in regard to everything it says about the essential properties of objects. One obvious case is that of the apple cited earlier. After all, an apple is the seedpod of an apple tree, so if it has any essential or important property it is that it contains seeds. But even here, it is possible to produce fruit that do not have seeds in them, as in the case of seedless watermelons. Nonetheless, having seeds remains the best candidate for an essential property of a fruit like an apple.

It's important to think about how you will handle the children's recognition that they don't agree with what the book says. One obvious point to make is that they all know the saying, "You can't trust everything you read." Well, they've just had a good example of its truth. You thus

Table 10.1. The Important Things about . . .

	A Spoon	*An Apple*	*You*
The important thing	You eat with it.	It is round.	That you are you.
Other things	It is hollow, etc.	It is red, etc.	You were a baby, etc.

have an opportunity to impress upon the children how important it is for them to be active and critical consumers of information. You might also stress that their training as philosophers will help them be able to make up their own minds about important questions rather than simply relying on what others tell them.

Depending on how long the discussion takes, you may or may not have time to raise the question of what the important thing about *you* is. *The Important Book*'s answer—that "you are you"—seems pretty difficult to endorse. If it means that everything about you is essential to your being you, then it's pretty clearly false. After all, I am still me even after I've shaved my beard, making me go from being a bearded man to a clean-shaven one. And similarly for many other properties. Nonetheless, the question of what makes you the very specific individual that you are is an interesting metaphysical question that it is fun to discuss with the children.

One version of this question is the problem of personal identity: What about you can be changed without making you into a different person? As I've said, it's pretty obvious that shaving a beard doesn't make you a different person. But you can ask the children to think about all sorts of different circumstances and whether the changes they envision would result in you no longer being the same person that you were. For example, what about losing a limb? Most of them would say that's not enough to change who you are. But what about not enjoying your favorite activity, such as playing the piano or playing ball? Would you still be you if you didn't like that activity?

Once again, it's important to realize that there are no certain answers to this, or indeed any, philosophical question. Philosophers continue to argue about what makes a person the person that she is. As I mentioned earlier, in order to try to support their views, philosophers often make use of weird science fiction scenarios that are called *thought experiments*. For example, if you and Albert Einstein (you can substitute the famous person of your choice here) switched brains using some advanced medical technique, which of the resulting beings would be you—the one consisting of Einstein's brain in your body or the one consisting of your brain in his body? Getting the children to think about such hypothetical cases is a good way to hone their philosophical skills. We'll delve into some of them in the next chapter.

THE IMPORTANT BOOK, BY MARGARET WISE BROWN

Questions for a Philosophical Discussion

A good way to begin discussing this book is to ask the children to make a chart with you on large paper or a blackboard like the one presented in table 10.1. With the children, you should go through some (or all, depending on time) of the objects that the books discusses and fill out the chart, listing the object, what the book says the important thing about the object is, what the book says other things that are true of the object are. Make sure to include one created thing like a spoon, one natural thing like an apple, and "you."

Once you've done this—or, perhaps, as you are filling out the chart—ask the children if they agree with what the book says. The idea is to get them to think about two things: First, is the book right in its classification of the important thing about an object? Generally, they will see that they don't agree with what the book said. Second, is there actually an "important thing" about the object in question? Here, they probably will at least disagree about what is really important about the things we have been discussing.

As the discussion progresses, you might ask them some of the following questions:

Topic: Artifacts and Essential Properties *The book says that the important thing about a spoon is that you eat with it.*

1. Have you ever seen a spoon that is not a spoon that you eat with?
2. What are some other things about spoons that are important?
3. Is there one "important" thing about a spoon? If so, what is it and why? If not, why not?

Topic: Organic Things and Essential Properties *The book says that the important thing about an apple is that it is round.*

1. What are some other important things about apples?
2. Is being round the important thing about an apple?
3. Could something be an apple and have some other shape?
4. Is there one important thing about being an apple?

Topic: Personal Identity *The book says that the important thing about you is that you are you.*

1. Tell us one very important thing about you.
2. Could you still be you and not possess that very important thing?
3. What makes you *you*?

11

THE WONDERFUL WIZARD OF OZ: TEACHING THE PHILOSOPHY OF MIND

The central question in the philosophy of mind is what makes human beings the unique creatures that they are. We all have bodies and also possess minds or consciousness. Are both of these essential to human beings? If not, can either one be thought of as some sort of complex aspect of the other? These are the sorts of issues that dominate this area of philosophical investigation.

The philosophy of mind is the area of philosophy that has been most affected by recent scientific discoveries. This is because scientists are figuring out more and more about the human brain and its relationship to conscious thought. Scientists are now able, for example, to localize certain emotions to specific locations in the human brain. This gives support to the philosophical position of *materialism*, the claim that consciousness is a complex feature of the brain but not something completely distinct from it, as *dualists* hold.

Another important issue in the philosophy of mind is that of personal identity, which concerns the question of what makes us the same person from one moment in time to the next, an issue that I already touched on in the last chapter. Different types of things have different "identity conditions." For example, a pile of leaves is usually thought to be the same pile only if all (or, perhaps, most) of the leaves in the pile are the same. If we replace the current pile with a whole new set of leaves, most people would agree that we now have a different pile, even though is in the same place as the first. This is because we think that the identity of the pile depends on its being made up of the same leaves or, to speak more abstractly, material constituents.

The issue becomes more complicated when we consider things that have more structure, say, a ship. The question of whether a ship can remain the same even though its constituent parts have changed was raised in ancient times through the story of the ship of Theseus. According to legend, the ship that Theseus used was preserved by the Athenians by replacing all of the decaying planks with new ones. The question that ancient philosophers debated was whether it could still be considered the same ship, despite the fact that all of its material parts had been changed.

A thought experiment can illustrate why this is a perplexing issue. In the story, the planks of the ship are replaced one at a time, so it is at least plausible to maintain that it is the same ship. But what if we burn the ship completely and then reconstruct it all at once out of different pieces of wood? Is it still plausible to say it is the same ship? Those who think that it is would argue that it is the sameness of the *structure* as opposed to the identity of the *material* that constitutes the identity of the ship, although others might claim that all we have is an exact *replica* of Theseus' ship and not the ship itself.

How does the problem of identity differ when it comes to human beings or persons? Well, for one thing, it is completely implausible to maintain that a person's identity depends on her being composed of the same material. Scientists tell us that all of the atoms and molecules that make up a human being get completely replaced every six years. (Although there is debate on the exact number of years, the general principle is certainly true.) So personal identity cannot be based on the identity of our constituent parts. But what about structural identity? Can this be the basis of personal identity?

It's not clear what the correct answers to these questions are. The existence of transplants and artificial body parts seems to suggest that identity of structure is a component of personal identity. What's important to realize, however, is that identity of structure cannot be the whole answer to the problem of personal identity. Philosophers have developed many peculiar and intriguing thought experiments to try to make this point. Consider, for example, the following story: Suppose that there is a new machine invented that can transplant one person's consciousness into that of another, memories and everything else included. Say that we now take you and Barak Obama and transplant your consciousnesses. Which, if either, of you *is* Obama?

There is a good case to be made that the person consisting of your former body and Obama's consciousness is Obama. Support for this view comes from the fact that the person consisting of your former body and Obama's consciousness has all of Obama's memories, dispositions, thoughts, and emotions, while the person consisting of Obama's former body and your consciousness seems more continuous with you. If that makes sense to you, then you would be endorsing the notion that identity of *consciousness* is what constitutes personal identity.

Of course, there are philosophers who deny that this is the correct answer. To justify their view, they also will put forward a thought experiment: Suppose that there is a consciousness duplicator, so that it is possible to replace one person's consciousness with that of another. Say that we use it to replace Obama's consciousness with yours, while you remain the same as you now are. Surely, these philosophers would say, we wouldn't be prepared to say that the entity composed of Obama's body and your duplicated mind is *you*, for you continue to exist. But this would show that a person's identity does not simply consist of the identity of his consciousness.

The story of the Tin Woodman from *The Wonderful Wizard of Oz* by L. Frank Baum (2000) is an excellent way to get children to think about issues of personal identity. This is the one story in our elementary-school philosophy course that comes from a chapter book and not a picture book. I have chosen to use it because I don't know of a picture book that raises issues in the philosophy of mind in such a clear and compelling manner. In addition, the popularity of the film version of the book means that many children will be familiar with the Tin Man, as the film calls him. Still, the book has only a few illustrations and that may make it harder to keep younger children entertained as you read them the story. One option would be to print some illustrations from the film and use them as you read the story to keep the children's interest. Another would be to show them a short segment of the film.

The Tin Woodman was originally a normal human being. But, as he slipped and cut off each part of his body because of the anger of the Wicked Witch of the East, a tinsmith replaced that missing body part with a tin version. By the end of the process, two things are true: First, although the Tin Woodman appears to be the same person as he was at the outset, there is no part of his body left from his earlier body. Second, although the Woodman is perfectly able to talk, he lacks both a brain and a heart. These facts provide the basis for our discussion of issues in the philosophy of mind.

Once you have read the children the chapter in the book called, "The Rescue of the Tin Woodman," you might begin your discussion by asking the children to explain how the Tin Woodman came to be made of tin. Once they have told you the story, you can ask them to tell you all of the ways in which the Tin Woodman differs from a normal human being, and you can make a chart of their answers (see table 11.1).

Once you have made the chart, the discussion can take different courses. One would be to ask the children whether the Tin Woodman is the same person that he was when he was in love with one of the Munchkin girls even though he's now made of tin. There are a number of factors that you can ask them to consider. One is that his body is completely different now, for all of his "fleshy" parts have been replaced with tin ones. Another is that he is incapable of feeling, according to the book, because he does not have a heart, which means that he no longer can feel the love that he had for the Munchkin girl. So he's clearly different. But he still thinks that he's the same person. Does that make sense?

Table 11.1. How the Tin Woodman Differs from Normal Human Beings

Features	*Tin Woodman*	*Normal Human Beings*
Arms, legs, etc.	Yes	Yes
Brain	No	Yes
Heart	No	Yes
Speaks	Yes	Yes
Walks	Yes	Yes
Made of	Metal	Flesh

Philosophers have been fascinated by the question of whether machines can think. Although this question is not directly raised by this story, the fact that all of the Tin Woodman's body parts are tin could give you an entry into this issue. The question would be whether only fleshy sorts of creatures are capable of having thoughts and feelings.

A further issue stems from the fact that the Tin Woodman lacks a brain and a heart. Since he can talk and act but not feel, this seems puzzling. You can ask the children what they think about this—that you need a heart to feel but not a brain to think. This leads into the Tin Woodman's claim that a heart is more important than a brain. Does this make sense? Are emotions like love more central to being a human being than thoughts? Is the reverse true? Are both equally essential? Is there something else that makes us what we are? All of these questions can contribute to the children having an interesting discussion of some of the basic issues in the philosophy of mind.

"THE RESCUE OF THE TIN WOODMAN" FROM *THE WONDERFUL WIZARD OF OZ*, BY L. FRANK BAUM

Questions for Philosophical Discussion

Topic: Personal Identity *"My body shone so brightly in the sun that I felt very proud of it"*

1. The Tin Woodman no longer has any of the body parts he did when he was a man. Do you think he is the same person he was before?
2. Would you be the same person even if your mind were put in your best friend's body? What if you could no longer play your favorite sport or instrument the way you could before?
3. The Tin Woodman cannot love the Munchkin girl because he has no heart. Does this mean he is not really the same person he once was?
4. What makes a person the same person at different times?

Topic: Brains versus Heart *Unlike the Tin Woodman, the Scarecrow wants to have a brain.*

1. Why does the Scarecrow want to have a brain?
2. Why does the Tin Woodman want to have a heart?
3. Which do you think is more important, brain or a heart? Why?

Topic: Happiness *"I shall take the heart," replied the Tin Woodman, "for brains do not make one happy, and happiness is the best thing in the world."*

1. What makes you happy?
2. What other things, besides happiness, do you think are good or valuable?
3. Do you agree with the Tin Woodman that happiness is the best thing in the world?

12

THE GIVING TREE: TEACHING ENVIRONMENTAL PHILOSOPHY

Philosophy is an ancient discipline, with roots extending back nearly three thousand years to ancient Greece. However, some areas of philosophical inquiry have only recently been recognized as suitable subjects for the serious thinking characteristic of philosophy. This is the case with environmental philosophy. Although any philosophical view of the world must necessarily include a way of thinking about the relationship between human beings and their environment, only in the last half of the twentieth century has this relationship been the subject of an ongoing philosophical debate.

The most obvious reason for the development of this new area of philosophical interest is the impact that advanced technology has had on human life on the planet. For the first time in the history of the human race, we have to face the possibility that our own actions may result in the destruction of many forms of life including, perhaps, our own, human one. This is a sobering possibility that has given rise to numerous social and political movements, from recycling to initiatives to reduce pollution and limit growth.

Philosophers have not been insensitive to the importance of this problem. So they have begun to focus their attention not only on current environmental concerns, but also on how the human-nature relationship has been theorized throughout the history of Western thought. The result has been a rethinking of the appropriate way for human beings to live their lives in a natural world whose resources are clearly finite and evidently dwindling.

One of the startling results of this new attention on the human-nature relationship is the realization that there has been a tendency in Western thought to think of the natural world as existing simply to be used by humans. The roots of this way of thinking extend back at least as far as the creation stories in the Old Testament, where God tells Adam and Eve that he has given them *dominion* over all the other beings in the world. What this biblical story means is that humans were intended to be the *rulers* of a world whose creatures and resources they were free to use as they saw fit.

Perhaps surprisingly, this view had no serious challenges within Western thought until the twentieth century. Even the radical critic of society Karl Marx (1818–1883) employed this way of thinking in his attempt to develop an alternative to the capitalist economic structure. He saw industrialization, with its ability to produce levels of material wealth never imagined in earlier epochs, as an unmitigated good, so long as it could be freed from the tyranny of private ownership. He never countenanced the possibility that what seemed like a great boon to humankind—technological innovation—might also contain the seeds of its own undoing, a possibility that we all now must face.

Once we begin to consider alternative roles for human beings besides that of being *rulers over the natural world*, the question of finding other ways of conceiving the relationship between humans and nature arises. One important alternative suggests that a more appropriate role would be as *caretakers* of a world that we have inherited and are to pass on to our descendents in such a way that they can likewise live fulfilling lives in concert with it. Accepting the notion that we are but caretakers of the natural world would have a huge impact on how we treat it. Instead of thinking of it as something simply there for us to use, we would have to think of ourselves as having an obligation to take care of it, to ensure its continued well-being. This would mean that we would have to undertake its preservation, treating it as something to which we often need to subordinate our own, more narrow interests and needs.

An example of such a caretaking role is the system of national parks in the United States. When Congress passed a law in 1916 setting aside such areas of wilderness, it outlawed development of areas of the natural world in the United States that had not yet been developed. One rationale for this was the need to preserve some wilderness for future generations, so that they could have a sense of what the natural world was like before the impact of humans and their technology. Although even this setting aside of natural areas has not been without its critics, it does provide one example of how an attitude of caretaking in regard to nature could affect our way of treating the environment.

Even if one accepts the idea that it is more appropriate for humans to think of themselves as caretakers of the natural world rather than as its rulers, there is lots of room for debate about what exactly this entails in relation to specific environmental policies. After all, we cannot live without using the natural world to preserve our lives. Even "low-impact" lifestyles require us to eat living things—even if only plants—and to consume other resources to clothe ourselves and keep ourselves sheltered. So we still have to ask questions about what the appropriate level of the consumption of resources is for humans and how we should go about justifying it.

Not all philosophers who reject the idea that humans have the right to make use of the natural world as they see fit would accept the idea that we ought to conceive of ourselves as its caretakers. An alternative view has been developed based on the idea that natural objects deserve our *respect*. The idea of respect is one that has had a fundamental role in ethics, but it has generally been employed to characterize the nature of our relations to one another. Indeed, our own rules for conducting a philosophy discussion make use of this notion by stating that the children should treat each other with respect. Applying this notion to the natural world has been an unusual move that is not without its problems, for few would agree that *every* natural object, even an annoying mosquito, needs to be respected!

There are other fundamental questions that also need to be resolved. One is whether nature or natural things have a value in themselves or whether their value comes from their relationship to human beings, the only beings that have intrinsic value. This problem can be illustrated in relation to our national parks example: Were these parks created because wilderness itself has intrinsic value, that is, is something worth preserving for its own sake? Or, alternatively, was it because wilderness has value in relation to human beings, say, as a place for them to recover from the strains of their everyday lives or as the source of a unique experience, that it should be preserved for future generations? This is an illustration of the sort of basic question that remains unresolved, even if one rejects the notion that humans have a right to do what they will with nature.

The question of the appropriate relationship that human beings should have with nature is raised by the story of a boy and a tree in Shel Silverstein's *The Giving Tree* (1964). In it, the boy's relationship with the tree undergoes a series of transformations. As a young boy, he climbs on the tree, plays with its leaves, swings from its branches, and eats its apples. The boy loves the tree, and the tree loves him. In a refrain that gets repeated later in the story, albeit with some qualification, we read, "And the tree was happy." But as they boy gets older, things change. As a young man, he wants money, so the tree gives him its apples to sell. When the boy then becomes a young adult, he wants to have a family and needs a house, so the tree tells him to cut its limbs to build the house. When the former boy returns to the tree as an older adult, disillusioned and wanting a boat, the tree selflessly tells him to take its trunk and fashion a boat out of it. When the boy does so, he leaves the tree barely alive, a mere stump. In the book's final episode, the boy returns as an old man, looking for a place to sit and rest. He finds it in the ever-faithful tree, now reduced to a mere stump.

In discussing this book with the children, our goal is to get them to think about the changing relationship with the tree that the boy has at different stages of his life. At first, although the boy uses the tree and its various features as a source for his enjoyment, he does so in a way that does not harm the tree. We might characterize the relationship this way: The young boy *respects* the tree and its *integrity*. But in the next three stages—that is, as a young man, a young adult, and an adult—the boy's relationship takes a more and more *destructive* course as he first takes the tree's apples to sell, then cuts down the tree's branches, and finally takes its trunk. When the boy returns as an old man, he takes up a less invasive relationship with what remains of the tree—its trunk—and simply sits on it and rests. It's not a stretch to take *The Giving Tree* to be a parable about different types of relationships that human beings can have with nature, and then to use it to initiate a discussion with the children about how humans *should* treat the natural world.

A good place to begin is with a chart of the different stages of the boy-tree relationship. If you set up the basic framework on both axes of the chart, the children will enjoy filling in all the rest of the boxes with you (see table 12.1).

Once you have finished making the chart, you should ask the children to discuss whether they think there ever is a stage when the boy does something wrong in using the tree as he does. There is room for a great deal of disagreement here, for some children might think that selling the apples is already problematic, while others will contend that even cutting down tree's trunk and leaving it a stump is fine. After you have canvased the children's opinions—perhaps by getting each of them to say if there is a time when the boy did something wrong and putting their names at the relevant stage—you should ask them to explain *why* they think that what the boy did at that stage was wrong but what he did at a prior stage was not.

Our aim here is twofold. First, we want to make sure that the children focus on the aspect of the story that is relevant for our discussion: that the boy's relationship with the tree changes from one that might be characterized as respecting the tree as an autonomous being to one that

Table 12.1. How the Boy Treats the Giving Tree

Stages of the Boy's Life	*What Does the Boy Do?*	*Why?*	*Is the Tree Happy?*
Young boy	Swings on the tree, etc.	Have fun	Yes
Young man	Sells the apples	Make money	Yes
Young adult	Cuts off the branches	Build a house	Maybe
Adult	Cuts down the trunk	Make a ship	No
Old man	Sits on the stump	Rest	??

?? indicates that children may have different views.

could be seen as exploitative and that certainly involves not treating it respectfully. Second, we want the children to see that, at a more general level, there are different ways in which a human being can relate to a natural object. This will prepare them for a more abstract discussion about the human-nature relationship, a topic that otherwise might be hard for them to get a handle on.

In moving to a more abstract level, you are going to be asking the children to see the story as a parable, though whether you want to discuss this with them depends on whether you think they can understand this concept. A parable is a story about specific characters that is intended to be understood as having a more general meaning or moral. *The Giving Tree* is a parable about how human beings treat nature. In teaching it, we therefore need to move from the specifics of how the boy treats the tree to the issue of how human beings should treat the natural world and all the objects within it.

Once you have gotten the children to propose some reasons for their views of how the boy acted—and remember, there need be no agreement at this stage, though there could be—you should ask the children to think about the general issue of how human beings should treat natural objects. You could ask them whether they think that the views they have about when and why the boy did something wrong in regard to the tree are also ones that they would endorse in regard to how people should treat all natural objects. Since this is a very abstract question, after telling the children that this is what they will be discussing, you will need to adopt one of a couple of different strategies for continuing the discussion.

One option would be to give them a more concrete question to deal with, such as whether it is all right to eat meat, although there are many other questions that you could ask that might be more appropriate in the context of your students. (For help on this, as other things, remember to refer to the question set that follows here.) Again, you need to get the children to explain why they think what they do, in addition to getting them to say what they believe.

Another alternative would be to ask the children if they would accept an ethical principle derived from their claims about the boy and the tree. For example, if one of the children said it was wrong to cut down the tree trunk because that meant the tree could no longer grow, you would need, first of all, to derive a general principle from this specific claim. So you might ask the children whether they think it is always wrong to do anything to a natural object that will cause it to no longer be able to grow. What about building a house? Or eating a fish? Odds are, they won't accept this general principle. If that's true, then they'll need to go back to the story and rethink what they've said. This can result in an interesting dialectic between general reasoning and the example on which it is based.

Using *The Giving Tree* to provide an example that will justify a general principle treats the book as a thought experiment. As we have seen, thought experiments are one of the most important techniques in philosophy, for they mobilize people's intuitions in a way that helps them decide what they think about general principles. Here, the story is a touchstone that can be used to get the children to formulate their views about the human-nature relationship. The benefit of using a thought experiment in this way is that it takes abstract theories down to specific cases about which it's easier to know what one thinks.

THE GIVING TREE, BY SHEL SILVERSTEIN

Questions for Philosophical Discussion

Topic: Giving and Altruism *The tree keeps on giving to the boy until it has nothing left to give, but the boy never gives anything to the tree.*

1. Do you think the boy is selfish? Why or why not?
2. What about the tree, is it selfish?
3. Is there a word for someone who keeps on giving without thinking about herself or expecting something in return?
4. Why do you think the tree is not happy after giving the boy its trunk?

Topic: The Nature of Giving and Gifts *In the story, the tree gives the boy many gifts.*

1. Have you ever given something away and later wished that you hadn't?
2. Is it easier to give something away if the receiver truly appreciates the gift?
3. When you give something to someone, do you expect something in return?
4. When you are given something, do you feel that you owe something to the person who gave you the gift?
5. Would you give something you really need to someone you love if they really need it, too?

Topic: The Nature of Love *Early in the book, we read that the tree loved the boy.*

1. Why do you think the tree loved the boy in the beginning?
2. Why do you think the boy loved the tree?
3. Are the two "loves" the same type of love?
4. Do people need to have a reason to love someone?
5. Do you treat people that you love differently from the ones that you don't?
6. When you love someone, how do you show her that you do?
7. Have you ever been angry with someone you love because she went away for a while, or because she did something you did not like?
8. Can you be angry with someone and love her at the same time?

Topic: Happiness *The tree is not really happy after giving the boy her trunk.*

1. Is the boy happy at the end of the story?
2. Is the tree happy?
3. If you were the tree would you be happy? Why?
4. Have you ever done something just to make someone happy?
5. Does doing things to make others happy make you happy?
6. Do you need a reason to be happy, or can you be happy for no reason at all?
7. Can you be happy and sad at the same time?

13

MORRIS THE MOOSE: TEACHING EPISTEMOLOGY

Whereas ancient Western philosophy took metaphysics and its interest in understanding the nature of what exists as the most basic field of philosophical inquiry, modern Western philosophy—which began in the early seventeenth century—is characterized by its view that epistemology is the fundamental philosophical discipline. Epistemology studies human knowledge. It seeks to establish the nature and extent of that knowledge. The reason that modern Western philosophers put epistemology ahead of metaphysics is that they believed we had to make sure that we were justified in our claims to knowledge before we could legitimately articulate the structure that reality had to have, for that structure could only be specified by means of knowledge claims.

Probably the most important figure for understanding epistemology is the skeptic. A skeptic is someone who denies that a particular type of knowledge is possible. For example, most people assume that they can know what someone else is feeling. But a skeptic about such knowledge argues that it is not possible to have knowledge about other people's mental states. After all, the skeptic points out, people often deceive us by pretending to feel something that they do not.

When you think that you know what someone else is feeling, you cannot really be sure—and certainty, the skeptic believes, is necessary for knowledge—that he is not pretending. Even if another person is crying and you think that he is sad, how do you know, the skeptic queries, that he is not deceiving you? You can't, the skeptic says, for we don't have the same type of access to the mental states of other human beings that we do in regard to our own. Hence, the skeptic concludes that we can never have knowledge of other people's minds.

There have been skeptical challenges to almost any type of knowledge that you can think of. For example, we all think that the sun will rise tomorrow (although we might not see it doing so, because of clouds or fog.) But have you ever thought about what basis you have for this belief? The most obvious answer is that you think this because that's what has happened every day in the past, and you have no reason to think that things will change tomorrow. But the skeptic argues that your assumption that the sun will rise tomorrow is not justified. How do you *know* that tomorrow might not be an exception, the one day the sun doesn't rise? In fact, almost every rule you can think of has had exceptions. Is there any way to rule out the possibility that tomorrow might be that exceptional day when there is no sunrise?

So far, we have seen the skeptic challenge both our knowledge of the feelings of others and also our expectations about the future. But the skeptic doesn't rest content with challenging only those beliefs. Virtually everything we think we know has been subjected to a skeptical challenge.

For example, another famous skeptical challenge asks how we each know that there is anything in the world other than ourselves. (This is more basic than the skeptical challenge in regard to the feelings and, hence, the minds of others, because it denies that you even have knowledge that you are actually looking at a page of paper when you have the experience of reading this book!) The kicker here is the "dream argument" made famous by René Descartes (1596–1650). He pointed out that all of us have had a dream that was so realistic that, while we were dreaming, we thought we were actually awake and not dreaming. Descartes, whose dreams were a lot more intellectual than mine, says that he dreamed that he was awake at his desk and writing when he was really asleep—but that he didn't know that he was just dreaming during the dream itself or even immediately after he awoke.

I think we've all had dreams like that, dreams from which we've awakened and not been sure that it was *just* a dream. Well, says Descartes, how do you know that you are not dreaming now? Couldn't everything that we take to be real simply be a dreamlike illusion, just as the deluded inhabitants of the Matrix world in the Wachowski brothers' film trilogy took the products of a computer program to be real things? How can you rule out waking up one day to discover that everything you thought was real was just a huge computer simulation?

Many philosophers take the central task of the epistemologist to be demonstrating why the skeptic is wrong. On this view, she needs to show why we are justified in claiming to know all the various things that we think we do: that there is a world "out there" inhabited by a variety of different types of things including people whose feelings we also know. However, many philosophers acknowledge the validity of some of the skeptic's challenges, so that we cannot salvage all of our everyday knowledge claims. For these philosophers, sorting out the legitimate claims to knowledge from the illegitimate is the task epistemologists have to deal with in the face of the skeptic's challenge.

Morris the Moose, the eponymous hero of Bernard Wiseman's book (1989), is not a skeptic. But he does have a mistaken belief, for he thinks that the other animals he encounters are all also moose. Normally, we think that it is easy to revise a mistaken belief that we have. All that we need to do is to acquire the appropriate corrective experience and we will realize that our beliefs were false and modify them appropriately.

In Morris' case, however, he has responses to all that the other animals say in their attempts to show him that his belief that they are moose is false. When the cow, for example, tells Morris that she moos in order to prove to Morris that she is a cow and not a moose, Morris is able to accommodate this fact into his belief system by responding that she is simply a moose that moos. From Morris' point of view, the cow is just an unusual moose, one that has an ability—mooing—that most moose lack. But she is a moose nonetheless. Morris can view any animal as a moose, so long as he is willing to adjust his concept of moose in such a way that all of the other animals' non-moosey characteristics are treated as simply unusual forms of "moosedom."

Willard Van Orman Quine (1908–2000), one of the most important philosophers of the twentieth century, argued that previous epistemologists had had an inadequate understanding of how knowledge worked. They had thought of human knowledge on the model of a building, which needs a secure foundation in order to support all that rests upon it. As a result, they had viewed our knowledge as also requiring a foundation. What they thought of as the foundation of human knowledge were some beliefs that were immune from skeptical doubt. A common view was that beliefs about our immediate experience—claims like "I'm now seeing a field of white with black letters on it."—constituted this secure foundation, for we could not be mistaken about this sort of thing.

Quine thought that this was a mistake, that the building analogy had misled philosophers into developing inadequate models of human knowledge. In place of that tired, old metaphor, he suggested that we should think of knowledge as more like an interconnected web with experience impinging on its edges. Sure, a new experience puts some stress on the web, but the web's flexibility ensures that it can be readjusted in different ways to accommodate anything that comes its way.

So instead of saying, as earlier philosophers had, that experience is the foundation of our system of knowledge, Quine argued that experience is just one factor that we use in establishing our beliefs about the world. As he put it (Quine 1961), any belief could be held onto—*even in the face of contrary experience*—so long as we make appropriate changes in our other beliefs.

In our story, Morris acts in one of the ways that Quine envisions: To maintain his belief that the other animals he encounters are all moose, Morris just readjusts his conception of what makes something a moose, allowing that there are all sorts of unusual types of moose. He has no problem, for example, admitting that moose can moo and give milk to humans. These are just the sorts of adjustments to Morris' beliefs about moose that are necessitated if he wishes to deny that the evidence presented to him by the other animals entails that they are not moose.

So our goal in this part of the discussion is to get the children to think about how someone can maintain a belief in the face of contrary evidence. We want them to think about the relationship of our beliefs, our knowledge, to the evidence upon which we base them. The story encourages them to see that there is no simple relationship between the two, that we don't have to react to contrary evidence by giving up our cherished beliefs.

Because the philosophical issues raised by *Morris the Moose* are quite complex, it's important to think carefully about how you might raise them with your students. (Before you read the book to them, you should make sure they know that the plural of moose is "moose.") One way to begin is to ask them, while showing them the picture of the cow, if they think that the cow looks like a moose. Presumably, they will say, "No." You can respond by saying something like, "OK, that's very interesting. But you know, Morris thinks the cow is a moose. Because he's a philosophically inclined moose, he always backs up his ideas with reasons. Do you remember what his reasons are for thinking that the cow is a moose?" (You can read them page 7 of the book again.) As they answer, you should put their answers onto the chart you make (see table 13.1).

You can then ask them why Morris thinks the fact that the cow has those three characteristics means she is a moose. If they immediately respond by saying that Morris thinks that anything that has four legs, a tail, and things on its head is a moose, you're set, for they have just put forward a general definition of a moose as being an animal with those three properties. If they don't immediately go there, you can ask them if those three things also apply to Morris, and thus moose in general. Once they realize that they do, you can then ask them why Morris makes the assumption that the cow is a moose.

Table 13.1, Is the Cow a Moose?

Why Does Morris Think the Cow Is a Moose?	*What Does the Cow Say to Show She's a Cow?*	*How Does Morris Respond?*
She has four legs.	Says she moos.	He can moo, too.
She has things on her head	Says she gives milk to humans.	She's a moose who gives milk to humans.
She has a tail.	Says her mother was a cow.	Her mother can't be a cow because she's a moose.

There are two ways to proceed once the children see that Morris thinks that having those three characteristics makes anything a moose. One might try to get the children to see that Morris made a very common mistake in reasoning. Here is the general pattern of his fallacious reasoning:

All As are B.
C is a B.
Therefore C is an A.

This is known as "the fallacy of affirming the consequent."

The philosophical field that studies the correct rules of thought is logic. It was first developed by Aristotle and remained more or less the same until the late nineteenth century, when it underwent a fundamental transformation initiated by Gottlob Frege (1848–1925), a German philosopher who worked in relative isolation and obscurity. It has now become a major area of philosophical research.

For our purposes, it's only important to realize that Morris' claim that the cow is a moose is based on a logical fallacy. Such fallacies are quite common in ordinary reasoning. Although logic can be a very technical mathematical field, it is based on the idea that it is important to establish norms for correct ways of reasoning.

Morris' reasoning goes awry in the following way: He begins with a true claim:

> All moose have four legs, a tail, and funny things on their head.

He also makes a correct observation:

> This animal has four legs, a tail, and funny things on its head.

Given the truth of the first statement, the following hypothetical statement is also true:

> If this animal were a moose, it would have four legs, a tail, and funny things on its head.

From this, Morris makes an invalid inference:

> This animal is a moose.

As I have said, this is an example of the fallacy of affirming the consequent. When one has a conditional statement—something of the form "If one thing is true, then something else is also"—it is a mistake to reason that if the something else is true you can know that the one thing is also. And that's exactly what Morris does.

Trying to get the children to see the fallacious reasoning that Morris employs can be difficult. If you are interested in trying, you might ask them what's wrong with the following inference:

> All peaches are fruit.
> This apple is a fruit.
> Therefore this apple is a peach.

They will know that something has gone wrong here and so will try to find an explanation for the problem.

An alternative way to proceed is to get the children to think about whether Morris is right to believe that anything that has four legs, a tail, and things on its head is a moose. To do this, you can ask them to say how the cow tries to show Morris that his reasoning is wrong. What the cow does is to point out three properties that she has that Morris lacks. The first is that she says "MOO!" The second is that she gives milk to humans. The final one is that her mother is a cow. The cow claims that all of these properties are true of her but not of moose.

At this point, you might ask the students if the cow is a good philosopher or not. More pointedly, you can ask them whether the cow is doing something that they also try to do when they are discussing philosophy. The answer is that the cow has tried to give Morris a *counterexample* to his proposed definition of a moose. The reason that the cow is a counterexample to Morris' moose definition is that, although the cow has all the properties that Morris says moose do, she also has some features that moose lack: mooing, giving milk to humans, and having a mother who is a cow.

Morris' responses to what the cow says show three different ways to respond to a proposed counterexample. First, Morris says that he can moo, too. This is a straightforward rejection of the claim that there is a feature of one thing that is not a feature of the other. A counterexample can sometimes be rejected because you don't think it really is a counterexample. That's Morris' first strategy.

Morris also uses a strategy that I have already mentioned. He revises his notion of moose. Before meeting the cow, Morris probably didn't think that a moose could give milk to humans. But now, confronted by an animal that he thinks is a moose and that does give milk to humans, Morris simply revises one of the features he thought was characteristic of moose. From now on, Morris would have to claim that there are two types of moose: those that give milk to humans and those that don't. Rather than rejecting his belief that the cow is a moose, Morris simply revises his notion of what a moose is.

Morris' final strategy is simply to deny the claim made by the cow, using his own belief to deduce the falseness of her assertion. Since he knows that the cow is a moose, he confidently asserts that her mother *could not be a cow* since she has a daughter who is a moose. Using one's own beliefs to deny the truth of what another says in an a priori manner is, unfortunately, all too often the way people respond to challenges to their beliefs. "That can't be true" may not be a good way to respond to counterevidence to one's beliefs, so it's worth discussing the validity of such a strategy with the children.

At this point, it's probably good to skip to the end of the story, when Morris and the other animals look at their reflections in a pool of water. You can ask the children why, after looking in the stream, Morris no longer thinks that the cow (or the deer or horse) is a moose. He actually supplies the answer directly: "You . . . do not look at all like me. . . . You cannot be [a] moose." (Wiseman 1989, 28)

Morris is now proceeding by means of the following principle:

> Two things that do not look at all alike cannot be the same type of thing.

This is actually a *metaphysical* principle and not an epistemological one, since it concerns the nature of things and not our knowledge of them, but let's not worry about that. Let's just try to get the children to think about whether they agree with it.

There are two issues here:

1. What determines whether two things look alike?
2. If two things look different, are they necessarily different *types* of things?

Let's think about each of these separately.

The first point we want to think about is whether it is possible to determine absolutely whether two things look alike or whether that determination depends on a context that must be assumed at least implicitly. To get your students to see this, you might show them three pictures—one of a painting of a man, one of a sculpture of a man, and one of a painting of a cow—asking them which two things look alike. The idea is, first, to see if some of the kids disagree about which two things look alike. If they do, ask them to explain why. If they all agree, say that you disagree. Then ask them to explain why they answered as they did and to say why they think you answered the way you did.

Our goal here is to establish that determining *likeness* or *resemblance* depends on the context one assumes in making the determination. If you are thinking about what the artwork is *of*, then the sculpture and painting of a man look alike in terms of their *subject*. But if you are thinking about the type of objects that they are, the two paintings look more like each other than either of them to the sculpture. Context here is everything!

The second thing we want the children to think about is whether Morris' implied principle mentioned above is valid. You can start out by asking them to think of other examples of Morris' principle. So they might say that a book and a pencil don't look at all alike so they must be different types of things. You might then pull an apple and a banana out of a bag, and ask the students whether they look anything alike. They will, of course, say no. But then you can ask them whether that means they aren't both fruit. They'll see that the principle does not hold in general.

But in the context of the book, the principle yields sound results. After all, Morris did come to the right conclusion using it. So you should follow up by asking when it is all right to conclude that two things that don't look alike are different types of things and when not. This is actually a real philosophical puzzle that the kids may enjoy thinking about.

One answer to this question is that *science* tells us when. That is, when science says that two things that look different are really the same type of thing, they are; and when science says that two things that look different really are different, they are. You might be able to get the children to see this by asking them whether steam and snow look at all alike. Or, even, snow and ice. Hopefully, they will say no but agree that they really are the same type of thing, namely, water. When you ask them how they know that, they may say that science explains it to them, for they both are composed of the same type of molecule.

One of the uncanny features of *Morris the Moose* is that the different animals—Morris, the cow, the deer, and the horse—sound like they are participating in a philosophy discussion. They each have different ideas that they put forward and discuss with one another in an attempt to convince the others that they are wrong. But they don't just say, "You're wrong and I'm right." They present what are in essence *arguments* to justify their views. And this is precisely what we are hoping the students will do in *their* philosophical discussions. So it's a very good idea to end your discussion of *Morris* by calling the children's attention to the philosophical character of the animals' discussion with one another. You can do this by asking them whether the way that the animals talk to one another reminds them of what they are doing in their philosophy lesson. Hopefully it will, and you can get them to explain exactly what features of the animals' discussion are philosophical.

MORRIS THE MOOSE, BY BERNARD WISEMAN

Questions for Philosophical Discussion

Topic: Beliefs and Experience *When Morris sees a cow, he thinks that the cow is a moose. When the cow says she's not a moose, Morris explains to her why he knows that she is one.*

1. What is the reason that Morris gives for the cow being a moose?
2. Explain the reasoning that Morris uses to conclude that the cow is a moose.
3. What is wrong with Morris' reasoning?

Topic: Knowledge and Truth *Morris thinks that he* knows *that the cow is a moose.*

1. Do you agree with Morris, that he *knows* that the cow is a moose?
2. Is there more to knowledge than having reasons for a belief?

Topic: Types of Knowledge *In order to explain why he thinks that the cow is a moose, Morris gives a reason for his belief, namely, that the cow has four legs, a tail, and things on its head.*

1. Give an example of something that you know for which you have a good reason.
2. Give an example of something you know for which you don't have a good reason.
3. How do you know the thing you said in response to question 2?
4. As a result of what you've now said, do you think that everything you know you know for a reason?

Topic: Persuasion *The cow tries to persuade Morris that she's not a moose, but a cow.*

1. How does the cow do this?
2. How does Morris respond?
3. Has anything like this ever happened to you?
4. Why do you think people keep saying they know something even though they don't?

Topic: Anger *When he sees Morris and the cow, the deer thinks they are both deer. When Morris hears this, he gets angry and yells at the deer.*

1. Does yelling make Morris right?
2. Why does he yell?

3. What do you think he should have done to convince the deer that he is wrong and that Morris is not a deer?

Topic: Sensory Experience and Belief *When the animals drink, they see their own reflections.*

1. Why does seeing their own reflections convince the animals that they were wrong?
2. There is a saying: "Seeing is believing." What might this saying mean? Do you agree with it?
3. Why isn't Morris convinced when the other animals tell him that he is wrong?
4. Can you think of other situations in which people have persisted in their mistakes despite having evidence that they are wrong?
5. Can you think of situations in which new evidence has made people change what they think?
6. Why is it so hard for Morris to admit that he made a mistake?
7. Do you think that people have a hard time admitting that they are wrong? Why is that?

Topic: The Nature of Philosophy *The animals all disagree with one another about who is what.*

1. When the animals disagree with one another, how do they try to convince each other that they are right?
2. What are the specific ways in which the animals talk to each other that remind you of how you discuss philosophy?
3. Are there differences between having a philosophical discussion and the way the animals disagree with each other?
4. Can philosophical discussions be settled by looking?

14

KNUFFLE BUNNY: TEACHING THE PHILOSOPHY OF LANGUAGE

Until the twentieth century, language was not a significant area of philosophical investigation. This was because, for many philosophers, thinking took place in the mind, and language was simply a vehicle people used to communicate ideas they had already formulated mentally. Language was, as philosophers like to say, *transparent*, something that functioned like a window, allowing ideas and thoughts to be transmitted but without making any contribution of its own.

Things changed fundamentally in the twentieth century, for philosophers began to see language as playing a crucial role in the very articulation of our thoughts and not merely as a diaphanous medium for their transmission. Philosophy of language therefore moved into the center of the philosophical landscape, for the contention was that language itself had to be understood before any of the other philosophical questions could be raised. Indeed, twentieth-century philosophers often transformed the traditional philosophical issues into questions about language. So instead of asking what made an action right or wrong, they would focus on questions about the language of ethical assessment, trying to understand, for example, how the word *ought* was used.

Once language is recognized to be of fundamental philosophical significance, a host of other important issues emerge. For example, the epistemological question of how our ideas are able to reflect the nature of the world gets recast as the question of how language is able to get a "hook" onto nonlinguistic reality. One of the central theories in the philosophy of language relies on distinguishing between two elements of a word's "meaning": its *reference* and its *sense* (Frege 1960). The idea is that words have a double sort of reality. On the one hand, they pick out objects and/or their properties in the world by *referring* to them. The word *rabbit*, for example, refers to actual rabbits on this view. But words also have a *sense*, something that is similar to what we ordinarily refer to as the word's meaning. The sense of *rabbit* would include such features as being furry and four legged, for these are features of the word that help us know what objects in the world it picks out.

Although this conception of language is one of the most important in the philosophy of language, many of its features have been challenged. For example, this account suggests that meanings can be attached to individual words just as a piece of luggage has a label with your name and address attached when you fly somewhere. But philosophers have argued that individual words do not possess meanings that can be attached to them in this way. Words acquire meaning, they assert, by reference to a range of similar concepts within a specific range. Thus, to say that a book is red is to also say that it is not green or blue, and so on. Color words acquire their meaning only through their role within a whole system. If this contention is correct, then meanings have a systematic structure that is not captured by the sense-reference theory of linguistic meaning.

There have also been philosophical skeptics about the entire concept of meaning. In a famous argument, Willard Van Orman Quine—whom we already encountered in our discussion of epistemology—argued that the concept of meaning is itself meaningless, that we would do better to dispense with it in favor of a more scientifically respectable notion founded on a theory of human behavior (Quine 1960). We could know the linguistic behavior of people, he asserted, but not what their words "mean." In his skeptical view, there is simply no fact of the matter about what our words really mean, for one could develop competing theories of linguistic usage that are equally well confirmed.

We have seen that one claim that has been hotly contested among philosophers of language is how language "hooks" onto the world. One theory of such a connection is *ostension*, or pointing. When we point at something while saying a word—such as saying "rabbit" as we point at one of the furry creatures—we are creating a word-world link. But other philosophers have argued that ostension already presupposes that we understand how to pick out one object from a range of other ones.

Think about someone standing in the door of a room looking in and just saying, "Look at that!" Without more understanding of the context, it is impossible to know what she is pointing out. Once we learn what the context is—that she is, for example, pointing to her favorite painting, which is just visible from the room's entrance—we will have a way of knowing what she is "ostending," but without the context we will be hard pressed to understand what object her statement is intended to pick out. This example shows why some philosophers believe that ostension presupposes the existence of a word-world link rather than explaining it.

Another fascinating issue is how children learn a language. It's amazing that children have the ability to acquire language on the basis of what is actually a rather limited range of evidence. Sure, parents generally spend a lot of time talking to their young children, but they often utter nonsense syllabus such as "Goo goo." How are children able to sort through this range of linguistic evidence and come up with an understanding of their native tongue relatively easily and quickly? This is one of the great mysteries of human life.

One of the simplest theories of language acquisition is that children simply have to learn what the "names" are for the "things" in their world. If we imagine a child to be a pint-sized adult—that is, equipped with a mature understanding of the world but simply lacking the knowledge of what word goes with what object—then this seems like a plausible view. A child's task, based on this view, is the relatively simple one of figuring out how to match words to their respective objects.

Once one reflects on the nature of language, the shortcomings of this view emerge. For one thing, it treats language as if it were primarily a map of the world, so that the child's task is simply to find the right labels for each of the objects that belong on the map. But philosophers have argued that a more fundamental role of language is coordinating our actions and understandings. Instead of seeing the most basic use of the word *slab* as a label for the large piece of slate in my vicinity, this view claims that the most basic use of the word would be in the command "Slab!" by means of which someone might get me to pick up the slab and put it on the pile of other pieces of this material where it belongs. The slogan for this view of language is "a word's meaning is its use," a view developed by another great twentieth-century philosopher, Ludwig Wittgenstein (1889–1951).

One very interesting issue is what features a symbol system needs to possess in order to actually be a language. One suggestion, presupposed by the "Slab!" example, is that a language must be understandable by more than one person. There cannot be—or, so many philosophers assert—a *private language*, a language whose essential characteristic is that one and only one person can understand it. On this view, language is an essentially social phenomenon that requires the existence of others in order to be mastered.

Another candidate is that a language must be capable of applying to new circumstances. Philosophers often call this feature of language its *generativity*, the fact that it can be used in situations that have never been previously encountered. You can, for example, understand all of the sentences in this book, even though you probably had not previously encountered any of them.

At an even more basic level, a language might be thought to require terms that refer to objects and others that refer to actions, although our "Slab!" example suggests that one linguistic item might be able to combine both of those functions.

One putative feature of a language that is *not* necessary is that it be made up of sounds. Sign language is a language, but it is composed of gestures not sounds. This is a useful example to keep in mind during the children's discussion.

Many of the issues about the nature of language that I have just enumerated emerge in the book *Knuffle Bunny* (Willems 2004). Knuffle Bunny is the name of Trixie's favorite stuffed animal. When Trixie goes to the Laundromat with her father, Knuffle Bunny gets left behind in the washing machine. Trixie's attempts to get her father to realize what has happened—"Aggle flaggle klabble!" she exclaims and does everything else she can to let him know how unhappy she is—are met with incomprehension. When they return home, Trixie's mother immediately asks where Knuffle Bunny is and her father realizes that the stuffed animal has been left behind. When Trixie in reunited with Knuffle Bunny, she utters her very first words: "Knuffle Bunny," as you might expect.

A good place to begin your discussion with children is with the rather obvious question of why Trixie is not able to communicate with her father. Of course, the answer—that she can't use language—is one the children will all agree with, but you can use their unanimity to initiate an inquiry into what Trixie knows and does not know. Clearly, Trixie cannot speak in the sense of uttering sentences, though she certainly can make noise. But can she think? She obviously realizes, in some sense, that Knuffle Bunny is missing, but when she says, "Aggle flaggle klabble!" is that baby-talk for "Help! Knuffle Bunny is missing"? Or is it more like her screaming "Waaaa!" as she does a few pages later? The issue here is whether young children are able to think, or whether they simply react to their feelings with sounds that are better assimilated to pain-expressing behavior like crying than to linguistic utterances.

To initiate this discussion, I suggest you ask the children to compare what Trixie is doing when she utters, "Aggle, flaggle, klabble!" and when she cries, "Waaaa!" It is helpful to show the two illustrations in which Trixie utters these "cries," because there are important features of each that the children might want to refer to in making their points. A good way to record their ideas is to ask them to fill out a chart (see table 14.1).

One way to move this discussion along is to raise the issues concerning ostension that I mentioned earlier. You might ask the children why Trixie's father doesn't understand that Trixie is trying to make him realize that Knuffle Bunny was left behind in the Laundromat. After all, Trixie might be thought to be saying something like "Stop!" Why isn't that enough to get her father to realize his mistake?

Table 14.1. Is Trixie Really Talking?

	When She Says, "Aggle, flaggle, klabble!"?	*When She Cries, "Waaaa!"*
Aim	Communication	Express her unhappiness
Content	Uses "words"	Doesn't matter
Accompanying behavior	Points, gestures	Additional gestures
What's in her mind	Thought (We left Snuffle Bunny behind!)	Feeling (unhappiness)

What we are trying to get the children to think about is what is distinctive about language as opposed to other forms of human behavior. We can and do communicate with others in various different ways. When someone cries, she often communicates a feeling of sadness, as one might by saying, "I am feeling sad." What we want the children to think about is what makes language such an important means of communication, as well as what the functions of language are.

As part of this inquiry into the nature of language, it would be good to raise the question of the relationship between thought and language. Some of them may think that Trixie has the thought that Knuffle Bunny is missing, but others will probably take her to be behaving in a way that is more like crying. It might be good, should this debate surface, to ask the students to think about how these different views could be compared and how we could decide if one or the other is a better theory.

The question of "theory choice," as this topic is called, is an important one in philosophy. Some philosophers hold that all theories can be compared in light of certain basic values, such as simplicity and explanatory power. But others hold that different theories are *incommensurable*, that there is no way to decide between competing theories, for there is no neutral standpoint from which to compare them. Getting the children to think about which view is better can be an interesting addition to this discussion about the nature of language.

A topic that we have found the children really enjoy discussing is what our lives would be like if we lacked a common language. We all know the biblical story of the Tower of Babel, in which God makes sure that human beings do not transgress the limits he has set for them by creating different languages so that the tower's builders cannot communicate with one another. You might ask the children what they would do if they couldn't talk to one another: How would they manage to play together? Could they find a way to get someone to do something simple, like pick up an eraser? This can turn into a fun game that will also bring to the children's awareness how fundamental a feature of our lives language is.

Since the basic assumption is that language plays a crucial role in human communication, you might ask the children what the necessary features of a language are (though not in those words!). You can ask them whether they think that there could be a language that only one person understood and that no one else could ever come to understand. You might also ask them whether they think a language has to be spoken or not. Using the example of sign language, you could also ask them to consider why that can be a language since it seems to consist completely of a person moving their body.

Sign language is a language that does not use sound. But it still has some elements of the structure that something must have to be a language. There are individual units of meaning, much like words, but that consist of gestures, such as placing both hands on one's heart to signify love. These gestures are capable of being combined into signifying units that express thoughts or make assertions, such as "I love you." Using the example of sign language will help the children to think about what a language is and how it works, the basic question raised in the philosophy of language.

KNUFFLE BUNNY, BY MO WILLEMS

Questions for Philosophical Discussion

Topic: The Nature of Communication *Before Trixie could even speak words, she went on an errand with her daddy to the Laundromat.*

1. How did Trixie communicate with her father before she could use words?
2. Could Trixie do anything other than cry to try to get her dad to realize her bunny was missing?
3. Have you ever had trouble communicating something to someone?
   a. What made it difficult?
   b. How did you solve the communication problem?
4. Why doesn't pointing help Trixie's father understand what's bothering her?

Topic: Language and Behavior *When Trixie realizes she left her favorite stuffed animal behind, she tries to tell her father through her actions.*

1. Are there some things that actions are better at communicating than words?
2. Does the way a person acts when they say something change how you understand what they are saying?
3. How do you know when someone is being silly or serious with their words?
4. Is language just as dependent on behavior as it is on words?

Topic: Meaning *When Trixie finally speaks, she says, "Knuffle Bunny!"*

1. There are lots of words that you haven't looked up in a dictionary, so how do you know what they mean?
2. Are there words or concepts that you just learned today? This year?
3. Does a blind person's idea of red differ from yours? Does she know what it means?

Topic: Language and Thought *Even though Trixie could not speak, she was still able to think about what she was trying to tell her father.*

1. How does language shape our thoughts?
2. When you learn more, can you think more?
3. Can you think without words?

Topic: The Nature of Language *Before Trixie could talk, she tried to communicate with her father through her own language.*

1. What is necessary for something to be a language?
2. Could there be a language that only one person could understand?

3. If your best friend didn't speak your language, could you still communicate with her (or him)?

Topic: Language and Animals *Trixie also tried to communicate with Knuffle Bunny.*

1. Do animals have thoughts? How can you tell?
2. Do animals have a language?
3. When a dog barks at something, is he trying to tell you something?
4. When you command your dog to "sit" and he sits, is this because the dog understands what you said?

15

EMILY'S ART: TEACHING AESTHETICS

Imagine that you had to judge an art contest for first graders. There would be drawings of all sizes, shapes, and styles. What criterion would you use to decide which piece should be awarded first prize? Should the picture of a house that really looked like a house be the winner? What about the drawing that showed how much a child loved her mother? And what of the very colorful abstraction that captured your eye with its striking design?

Emily's Art, an imaginative picture book by Peter Catalanotto (2001), raises just such questions. In it, Emily is a highly talented young artist whose pictures, though not realistic in any obvious sense, are skillfully done and express her thoughts and feelings about whatever she draws. A painting of her mother, for example, has multiple images of her mother to show how busy she is preparing everyone's breakfast, and in a painting of her dog, Thor has huge ears because he hears so well.

As we read the book, we see how talented Emily is as an artist as we come to appreciate her nonrealistic style of drawing. Everyone in Emily's school knows she's the most talented artist in the class, because, like her best friend Kelly, they often come to her to ask advice about their drawings. So when Emily loses the school art contest because she has entered Thor's picture and the judge dislikes dogs intensely, the question of how we should judge works of art emerges intensely for the book's readers. The children's usual response to the judge's decision is simply, "That's not fair." But exploring why it's not fair leads into an interesting discussion of how we make judgments about the quality of works of art.

Aesthetics is the branch of philosophy that is concerned with questions about art, although its purview is larger than that, extending to a range of questions about our appreciation of things like nature. For our purposes here, it will be adequate if we get a sense of the basic questions about art that aesthetics focuses upon.

The central aesthetics question raised by *Emily's Art* is that of whether there are objective standards for the evaluation of works of art. Philosophers disagree about this basic issue. Some argue that there are such objective standards. The grounds for this view are varied, but some have to do with what we ordinarily think about art. Museums are often taken to be repositories for the great art of the past. But if we claim that certain works are *great*, aren't we committed to the notion that there are objective standards that we use to justify their greatness? It seems that we have to have some grounds for making our standard evaluations of works of art other than our own subjective experience of them.

Of course, there are philosophers who are skeptical about the existence of such standards. What, they ask, could possibly count as such a standard? One of the differences between art objects and other things is that there are no specific properties that always make an artwork good. Think about *having detail*, a criterion often proposed as a "good-making" feature of works of art. Although we might admire a painting by Rembrandt for the meticulousness of its detailed rendering of a gold chair, the accumulation of detail in another work might be judged to make it fussy, a term of evaluative disparagement. According to such skeptics, there are no objective criteria that can be used to evaluate works of art.

But, you might counter, doesn't this make all evaluation of artworks pointless? Sure, a critic might tell you that he likes this painting or film, but all that would mean is that it appeals to him. He couldn't tell you that it was great or even good, for such terms seem to imply the existence of objective standards.

A response might begin by pointing out that such a situation might make sense when we are simply talking about our own reactions to things like foods. One person might prefer chocolate ice cream to vanilla, for tastes are merely subjective, nothing about which there can be argument. You get to be the arbiter of your own tastes, and no one can convince you that you are wrong. But making claims about the merit of works of art is different, for we do think that there must be some standards to justify our evaluations of them.

One piece of evidence for this contention is that we think that it makes sense to have critical arguments. While we would just laugh at someone who tried to convince us that we liked vanilla ice cream better than chocolate when we told them the opposite, we think it makes perfect sense for critics to argue whether Van Gogh's *Lily* is a better painting than, say, Whistler's famous portrait of his mother. But if there can be rational disagreement about the evaluation of works of art, then it would seem that there would have to be objective standards by which such disagreement could be adjudicated.

To this, the skeptics would respond by saying that those who think that there are objective standards of artistic evaluation fail to consider the importance of artistic experts, that is, critics, artists, art historians, and the like. All that these critics can base their assessment of works of art on is their own experience. When they disagree with each other, they are not just trying to bully the other into submission, however. Their goal is to get the other to see what they see, to experience what they experience. So, if a critic says that Van Gogh's painting is better than Whistler's, he'll point to different features of Van Gogh's painting in order to help those who disagree with him notice how those features contribute to *Lily* being the great work he thinks it is, that is, one that causes him to experience the intense sort of pleasure that art can.

In discussing *Emily's Art* with children, our goal is to get them to think about the issue of artistic evaluation, to puzzle over whether there are objective criteria by means of which we evaluate artworks. But we can't start out right there. It's better to begin by asking the children to evaluate Emily's works, which are scattered throughout the book. For example, you might start out with the picture of Thor, the one Emily enters into the contest, and ask the children to say what they like about it.

You can also ask the children whether they think it is a good painting or not and why. You might then turn to Kelly's painting of a butterfly and ask them the same question. Once again, it might be useful to record their observation in a chart. (See table 15.1)

Beginning with this comparison between characters' paintings serves a couple of purposes. First of all, it is something that each child can take a stab at answering without any prior knowledge about art. It would be a mistake to think that all children have had very much exposure to art other than that which they make. Starting with the two drawings helps acclimate all the children to discussing a topic that they may feel is one they don't have much to say about.

Second, such a comparison can produce a set of criteria that might function as a basis for evaluating works of art. For example, some candidates for things that were proposed by a group of fifth graders at the Jackson Street Elementary School for why Emily's picture was "good for a first grader, but not something I'd want to hang in my room or pay $1,000,000 for or anything" was that it had detail and interesting colors. As we'll see, getting such specific standards of artistic merit out on the table will be helpful in the later discussion.

If the children haven't discussed Thor's ears, it might be useful to follow up by asking the kids why they think Emily gave Thor such long ears. The book actually has the answer: because he hears so well. But it might be worth asking them if they like paintings that are more realistic—you could even bring in a realistic rendering of a dog and have them discuss which painting they think is better. (If you do this, you could add a column to the chart for this picture.) This would allow them to enter into a critical discussion of the relative merits of two paintings, Emily's and the realistic one.

Table 15.1. Comparing Emily's Painting with Kelly's

	Emily's Painting	*Kelly's Painting*
What is it a painting of?	Thor, her dog	A butterfly
Is it a good painting?	Yes	??
What do you like about it?	Colorful, detailed, expressive	Looks like a butterfly
What don't you like?	??	Not original or imaginative

?? indicates that children may have different views.

In order to prepare the ground for the more abstract discussion, you could now change the subject a bit—after marking what has been established, of course—by asking the kids whether they prefer chocolate or vanilla ice cream. Once they have all had a chance to answer, you can ask them to explain why they like one better and whether they think that they are right about what they think.

This will initiate a discussion about the nature of tastes, one that will presumably result in their agreeing that "there is no disputing taste," as the famous saying goes. The case of tastes, in which it seems evident that there is no objective standard for our claim to like one more than the other, will form the contrast case to judgments of artistic merit, where we don't just say that we prefer one painting to another, but say that one is better. We are here preparing the ground for the later discussion.

Now you are ready to ask the big question: Do you think there is any difference between saying that you like chocolate ice cream better than vanilla and saying that Emily's drawing is better than (or worse than) the realistic one? Since, as we have seen, philosophers disagree about the answer to this question, we can expect that the children will as well. So one thing that you can do as a facilitator is to play devil's advocate or, at least, try to draw each position out of the answers the children give.

The fifth graders I just referred to did a great job of setting up the disagreement. One student said that he thought that there was no difference between the case of taste and the case of art: "When I say that Emily's painting is good, it's just like saying I like chocolate. The two cases are the same." In order to get the other position developed, the facilitator asked the fifth graders, "When a judge judges works of art, how does she do it?" To which another student responded by saying that the judge can't just use her own preferences. "Otherwise," he continued, "people will just draw for the judge. If she likes windmills, then everyone will just paint windmills. A judge has to judge on the basis of features of the pictures, like their having detail or interesting colors. She can't just use her own taste."

One of the difficulties of leading a philosophical discussion among children that I already pointed out is being content with a disagreement. So much teaching involves asking the children to come up with the *right*

answer that it can be difficult to feel good about having a discussion that doesn't reach a clear resolution.

It's important, however, to realize that this is what usually happens in professional philosophical discussions. Philosophers simply disagree about most of the fundamental questions they address. As I said, although many philosophers think that there have to be objective criteria of artistic evaluation, others simply reject that notion as ill founded. In teaching philosophy, you have to get used to the idea that disagreement, if it is expressed respectfully and courteously, is a good thing, not a bad one.

On the other hand, it is very important to make sure that the children realize that they have accomplished a lot even if they have not *solved* the problem that was raised. To do this, you can do two things.

The first is to say, as I just have, that disagreeing is one of the things that philosophers do. But, second, you should point out that what the children are now disagreeing about is a very sophisticated point that they have themselves reached by means of the discussion. It's important for them to realize that understanding an issue in a more sophisticated manner is at least as important as coming to a resolution of it. So point out to them how far the discussion has come, perhaps by going over the course of its development.

Emily's Art raises other philosophical questions that you should feel free to discuss as well, especially if the children are interested in them. An obvious one is what makes an action fair or just. The judge's awarding first prize to Kelly is a clear case of an unjust action, so it would be easy to initiate a discussion of fairness—one of the basic concepts of social and political philosophy—by means of this incident. Another feature of the story is the friendship between Emily and Kelly. Since the two are "best friends," you could initiate a discussion of what makes someone your best friend or, more generally, why it is important to have friends. The concept of friendship has received attention from moral philosophers all the way back to Aristotle, so it is an eminently suitable subject for a philosophical discussion. Letting the discussion go where the children want to take it is more important than making sure that they understand the issue about aesthetic merit.

EMILY'S ART, BY PETER CATALANOTTO

Questions for Philosophical Discussion

Topic: The Nature of Contests *In this story, Emily's school has an art contest and the students discuss different kinds of races.*

1. Who has been in an art contest?
2. What other types of contests have you been in?
3. Does a contest always have to be a race?
4. Have any of you ever seen a science fair?
5. How is a winner decided in a running race? Science fair? Art contest?
6. Are there differences between a science fair and a foot race—even though both have a winner? If so, what are they?
7. Does the judging/winning differ between the two? If so, how?
8. Is one contest easier to judge than the other? If so, how?

Topic: What Is Art? *In this story, Emily's artwork was not chosen as the winner of the art contest.*

1. What are some things that you consider to be art?
2. What makes something a piece of artwork?
3. Does art have to be man-made?
4. What makes someone an artist?
5. What does one have to do in order to be considered an artist?
6. Can anyone be an artist?

Topic: Evaluating Art *In one of Emily's paintings she has four mothers. She said it was because her mother is so busy in the morning.*

1. What does Emily mean when she says this?
2. What is special about her paintings?
3. Because Emily's paintings are not the way things are in real life, are her paintings not as good as other paintings? Why or why not?
4. Who should be able to determine whether a painting is good or not?

5. What happens if two people disagree on whether or not a piece of artwork is good?

Topic: Art Expertise *In order for a winner to be chosen in the art contest, there has to be a judge. The judge in* Emily's Art *is the principal's mother. The judge explains that she is qualified to be the judge of the contest because her cousin is married to an artist.*

1. Does being the principal's mother make someone a good judge? Why or why not?
2. Should there be a special person to be the judge of an art contest?
3. How should the judge be chosen?
4. How should the judge choose which painting is the best?
5. Does the painting that wins the contest have to be realistic or pretty?

Topic: The Nature of Feelings *Emily goes to the nurse when she's not feeling well. The nurse asks her what's wrong.*

1. Does Emily's heart literally hurt? If not, what does Emily mean when she says that she had hurt her heart?
2. Have you ever had your heart hurt?
3. Why does Emily's heart hurt?
4. How is hurting your heart different from hurting another body part, like your leg?
5. Is the healing process different for each type of hurt/pain?

Topic: Art Interpretation *The judge loved Emily's picture when she thought it was a rabbit but when Emily's teacher told the judge it was a dog, she changed her mind and chose another picture.*

1. Why does the judge change her mind and choose another picture?
2. Is this how a picture should be judged?
3. Should it matter that the judge viewed Emily's painting as one thing, and Emily had something else in mind?
4. Is it possible to know what an artist was thinking when he painted a picture?

IMPLICATIONS

16

SUGGESTED FOLLOW-UP ACTIVITIES AFTER PHILOSOPHY DISCUSSIONS

To this point, my focus has been on helping you prepare for philosophy discussions that you can facilitate in a single session with your students. In part, this is because this is what both my students and I have experience doing. We generally visit classes to lead philosophy discussions that need to be completed in just one visit. But it's also because leading a learner-centered discussion is likely something that is different for you. As a result, I thought it important to give you a clear sense of what is required for this style of teaching. Additionally, because philosophy may be a field that you are new to, I wanted to spend some time explaining the nature of philosophy and how specific children's stories raise philosophical issues.

But it would be a shame if you let your students' engagement with a philosophical issue drop after just a single discussion. After all, philosophy discussions generate a lot of excitement for the children. Why not use that excitement to fuel their learning in other ways? Indeed, part of the value of introducing philosophy into elementary-school classrooms is its potential to enliven many different aspects of the curriculum.

There are many ways in which this can be done and I'm sure you will have many ideas of your own. So let me just mention a couple of obvious ones. Since the children have been deciding what they think about a philosophical issue and what their reasons are, you could ask them to write a short explanation of their ideas. The goal of such an exercise would be to have the students present their ideas clearly and support them in a logical fashion. These are, after all, the central aims of expository writing, so philosophy discussions can be a good means for developing the students' skills in this area.

Some students may not be ready to write a philosophical essay, even a very short one. Such students can still take part in various types of follow-ups. You might ask them to draw something that represents ideas they got out of the discussion. With *Emily's Art* (Catalanotto 2001), for example, you might ask the students to make a drawing in Emily's expressive style. But even books about more abstract topics can have drawing follow-ups, as you can see from the specific suggestions given in the following pages.

You can also develop games for the students to play that elaborate on the ideas raised during the discussions. Asking them to communicate with one another without using words, as we do in our follow-up to *Knuffle Bunny* (Willems 2004), can develop their understanding of language.

The children's oral-language skills as well as their ability to cooperate can be improved by asking them to take part in debates. You can separate the students into small groups and ask each group to defend a position on one of the issues that has been discussed. For example, you could stage a debate about whether writing poetry should count as doing work or not. Since the children will have already discussed this issue together and heard arguments on both sides of the issue, it will be easier for them to develop arguments in support of the position they are assigned.

Writing a poem about a question they have discussed is another option that would allow students with different proclivities to develop their philosophy lesson in an interesting direction. You might ask them to adopt the point of view of the tree in *The Giving Tree* (Silverstein 1964) and write a poem expressing its feelings at one stage in its relationship to the boy.

Below, you will find some examples of follow-up activities that the teachers at the Martin Luther King Jr. Charter School of Excellence have used with their students. Try out some of these or be creative and develop your own follow-up activities. You'll see how philosophy can be the trunk of the tree of learning with many diverse and varied branches growing out of it.

SUGGESTED FOLLOW-UP ACTIVITIES

1. For "Dragons and Giants": Ask the students to draw someone they think is brave and/or describe why the person is brave.
2. For *Frederick*: In the book *Frederick*, the field mice go to live in the cave during winter. While in the cave, the mice run out of food and Frederick uses the art of poetry to help pass the days. Now it is their turn to create their own suitcase for the winter. Ask them to think of *four* things that they would bring to survive the winter that resemble the field mice's supplies and *one or two* things like Frederick's. Have the kids draw pictures that represent what they think are the most important things they will need to survive a long winter. Remind them to be very thoughtful and careful in their selection, because they will have to explain why they picked each item.
3. For *The Important Book*: Ask the students to choose any item in the classroom, list some of its properties, and explain whether or not it has one "most important property." Or pair up your students. Ask them to interview each other and then to create a page like the ones in the book that list all the properties of their partner, including the most important one. They can even draw a picture of their partner.
4. For *The Giving Tree*: Have the students draw or write something that they think the old man could have done with the stump that would have been better than just sitting on it.
5. For *Morris the Moose*: Ask the children to draw pictures of two things that look different but are really the same underneath.
6. For *Knuffle Bunny*: The following exercise is meant to get children thinking about whether it is always better and more successful to use words or gestures to communicate. Have the children form a circle around you. Place the book on the ground and tell the group that one at a time, they are to give you *one* direction on how to pick the book up off the ground. The children can only use their words;

no hands or gestures are allowed and only one instruction per person. As the teacher, make sure to take everything they say literally, as if you are a robot that has never picked up a book before. The objective is to show children how much we as humans rely on body language and gestures to communicate. After the children, working collectively, get you to pick up the book, have them reflect on the exercise by asking the following questions: What did you learn? What did this exercise show us about communication? Have your thoughts or opinions changed?

7. For *Emily's Art*: Have the students make a drawing that expresses their feelings about something.

17

CONCLUSION

One day, my three-and-a-half-year-old son, Jake, had finished watching a video. I decided that he had watched enough for now and told him he couldn't watch another one. He really wanted to, so he asked me, "Why?" I told him that two videos were too much. He thought about this for a while, puzzled. After a moment, he looked at his hand and held up two fingers. "Daddy", he asked, "are these too many fingers." "No," I replied. "Then two videos are not too many videos," he asserted. I was so surprised at a three-year-old child's ability to make this analogical argument, unsound as it was, that I let him watch another video.

I mention this story for two reasons. First, I think it demonstrates yet again that children are natural-born philosophers, interested in discovering the power of rational thought and eager to use it in many aspects of their lives. But I also think it shows what can happen to children when we allow them to be the free and independent thinkers they aspire to be: They can use the skills we have fostered in them in ways that we may not always find suit our own adult agendas. If we really want to give our children the freedom they want and deserve, including the freedom to pursue their philosophical interests and to develop their argumentative skills, then we have to reckon with young children who are more assertive, more intellectually independent, and less pliable than children have traditionally been taken to be by their teachers and parents.

Although this may be a scary prospect to some, it should not be. The philosophically sophisticated children who come out of our philosophy for children program may require us to give them reasons for what we want them to do more often that other kids do, but if we step back and think about what this means, we can only be gratified, for their very orneriness is exactly what we want to foster. For among other things, one of the reasons why we want to introduce young children to philosophy is the hope that doing so will foster their inquisitiveness and help them develop their own independence of thought. The success of our attempt will result, in part, in our finding ourselves confronting children who are less pliant, less willing to simply do as they are told, and who want to know more often why they should be doing what we are asking them to.

I want to emphasize that I believe this to be a genuinely good result. If we only had a nation of adults who once had been philosophically sophisticated children, what a difference it might make. Think about what the world would be like if all adults had a solid background in philosophy from their elementary educations! "Politics as usual" would, for the first time, really have to change, for citizens would no longer put up with the rationalizations they keep getting asked to accept. Our workspaces would change, for workers would be ready to engage in dialogue with their supervisors about the structure of their jobs. Advertisers would have to reckon with a more critical and demanding public. It's hard to know where this would end, how far-reaching the impact of widespread philosophical educations would be!

So as you decide to take some tentative steps at initiating philosophical discussions among children, realize that you are part of a worldwide social movement that could have dramatic impact on human life on this planet. As each of us does what he or she can to foster philosophically sophisticated young people, we are working toward the broader goal of not only giving each young person the chance to develop an important natural interest they have but also fostering the development of a more reasonable society and world.

I hope that this book is only the first step in your ongoing engagement with teaching children philosophy. I have focused on providing you with a step-by-step guide for beginning to discuss philosophy with young children. Many of the specific features of what I have suggested are intended to make engaging in philosophical discussions with young children something that would not be difficult to do. For this reason, I have advocated using a pretty standard methodology with a number of specific steps to it.

Once you become comfortable talking with children about the philosophical issues that they find interesting you can, to use Wittgenstein's (1953) famous metaphor, throw the ladder away. That is, once you've been helping children discuss what makes something the right thing to do or how they know that they are not dreaming now, you will find that you can engage them in philosophical discussions based on children's books without having to go through many of the specific steps I have described in this book. Just as children are natural-born philosophers, we all have it in us to become skilled facilitators of philosophical discussions.

You can avail yourself of many other resources as you continue to develop your skills as a facilitator of philosophy discussions. I have assembled a number of these in the appendix. I hope you find them useful.

You'll recall that I began this book with what might have seemed like an outlandish claim: that children are natural-born philosophers. By now, I hope you're convinced that it is not at all an exaggeration. And if you've tried using what I've provided you with to actually initiate philosophical discussions with young children, I'm certain you'll agree with me. In fact, I expect that the children will have an easier time convincing you of their philosophical potential than all of the evidence I could ever muster. Seeing is believing, as the saying goes, and nothing surpasses the amazement you'll experience when you actually witness a child making an insightful philosophical claim. As I told you at the outset, it was my experience with children that convinced me that they deserve to have the opportunity to discuss philosophy in their classrooms.

If you use this book to help bring philosophy to the lives of elementary-school children, you will be doing them—and our society—a big favor. You also will be opening yourself up to one of the most wonderful experiences I have had, for children can reacquaint you with the pure joy of a first encounter with philosophy, that ancient form of reflection on the nature of what it is to be a human being on this strange, funny, and frustrating globe on which we find ourselves.

APPENDIX

Suggestions for Further Investigation

The appendix contains a variety of different suggestions for continuing your investigations into discussing philosophy with children. It includes books, articles, and websites that I have found useful in my own work with kids,

To aid others' attempts to discuss philosophy with children, I have developed the website www.teachingchildrenphilosophy.org. The website has two parts. The first part contains *book modules* for a wide range of children's books. You'll recognize a book module as having a similar structure to the chapters of this book that focused on individual books and specific philosophical topics. Along with a short summary of the children's book, the modules have both a short introduction to the philosophical issues raised by the book and a set of questions to use to initiate philosophical discussions among young children.

Most of the book modules on the site have been developed by undergraduates in my philosophy for children course. Every year, I ask each of them to choose a children's book that they think is philosophically interesting and to develop a module that they will put up on my website. So the list of books we have available for you continues to grow each year.

We have made the site as user friendly as we can. In addition to a listing of the books in alphabetical order, we have grouped them by philosophical field (such as ethics or metaphysics) as well as by more specific subject (such as bravery or essentialism). I hope that you will take advantage of the site and use the materials it contains to teach a wider range of topics than I have been able to include in this book.

You'll even find some book modules for chapter books on the website. Children in the older elementary grades are able to read these books by themselves, so you can continue to have philosophical discussion with older children by using them. I have been able to structure lessons around short chapter books like *The Real Thief* (Steig 2007) with children as young as second graders. This requires integrating philosophy time into the curriculum on a more frequent basis, since the books take longer to read and understand. But, once again, the results are truly heartening.

In addition to the book modules, the website contains almost all the materials I use in teaching my course. I have put them there so that anyone who is interested in teaching a similar course can freely borrow from what I have developed. When I set out to develop this course, I was unable to find any models to use in creating it. I hope that what I have placed on the website will make it easier for others to develop similar courses. It goes without saying that you should borrow what you want and ignore what you don't.

Here is a list of books and articles about philosophy for children that I have found useful in my own work. I recommend them to you.

- *Teaching Thinking*, by Robert Fisher (2008), has both a theoretical brief for introducing philosophy into elementary schools and a lot of practical advice.
- David Kennedy's *The Well of Being: Childhood, Subjectivity, and Education* (2006) is a theoretical brief for doing philosophy with children.
- Matthew Lipman has written many books both for and about doing philosophy with children. His most comprehensive statement is *Thinking in Education* (2003).
- Gareth Matthews has written three books about philosophy for children. All of them are useful. *Philosophy and the Young Child* (1980) explores the ability of young children to discuss philosophi-

cal ideas. *Dialogues with Children* (1984) is a record of a number of conversations that Matthews had with children at St. Mary's Music School in Edinburgh, Scotland. It vividly demonstrates children's ability to discuss philosophy. *The Philosophy of Childhood* (1994) is a more theoretical work that examines many of our unfounded assumptions about children.

It is hard to find an introduction to philosophy that is really useful for developing a more substantive knowledge of the field.

- My students love Thomas Cathcart and Daniel Klein (2007), *Plato and a Platypus Walk into a Bar . . . : Understanding Philosophy through Jokes.* You should realize that although this book presents different philosophical positions on a range of issues in a witty and entertaining manner, it does not explain the nature of philosophical reasoning.
- A longer but more satisfying introduction to philosophy is *Looking at Philosophy: The Unbearable Heaviness of Philosophy Made Light* by Donald Palmer (1994).
- A very good, short introductory text is Thomas Nagel's *What Does It All Mean?* (1987).
- The online Stanford Encyclopedia of Philosophy (plato.stanford .edu) has in-depth articles on most philosophical topics. It is a refereed online resource, so it is trustworthy. However, the articles are often quite difficult because they are addressed to professional philosophers.
- There is a radio show run by two professional philosophers from Stanford called *Philosophy Talk*. They interview guests on a wide range of philosophical issues. Their website allows you to listen to any of their previous programs: www.philosophytalk.org. My students have found this a good way to begin their introduction to various areas of philosophy.
- A novel that is also a very popular introduction to the history of philosophy is Jostein Gaarder's *Sophie's World* (1991).

Here is a list of websites that can be helpful to you. Be warned, however, that websites are ephemeral creatures: They come and go quickly, often with no warning and leaving no trace. All I can say is that all of these were alive and kicking when I finished writing this book.

- The Institute for the Advancement of Philosophy for Children (IAPC): cehs.montclair.edu/academic/iapc/
  This is the place where it all began. Founded in 1974 by Matthew Lipman, the IAPC focuses on teacher trainings as well as coordinating philosophy for children worldwide.
- The International Council for Philosophical Inquiry with Children (ICPIC): www.icpic.org
  ICPIC aims to strengthen communications among those in different parts of the world who are engaged in philosophical inquiry with children. The website includes links to many other sites.
- Northwest Center for Philosophy for Children: philosophyfor children.org
  There are a variety of resources on this site that are useful in developing philosophy lessons. The center also offers a variety of different activities for those interested in teaching philosophy to young people.
- UK Society for the Advancement of Philosophical Enquiry and Reflection in Education: sapere.org.uk
  This site has a guide to philosophy for children's activities in the United Kingdom.
- Philosophy for Children—New Zealand: p4c.org.nz/
  This website has a guide for introducing philosophy into the curriculum with focus on New Zealand and includes a listing of events and trainings.
- Philosophy for Kids: University of Massachusetts: www.philosophy forkids.com
  This website is focused on allowing children to do philosophy by finishing or beginning stories that are philosophically interesting.
- Wondering Aloud: philosophyforchildren.blogspot.com/
  This is a blog focusing on philosophy for children developed by Janet Mohr Lone, director of the Northwest Center for Philosophy for Children.
- Kids Philosophy Slam: www.philosophyslam.org

This site presents contests on specific areas that children can enter to test their philosophical skills.

- VisioNaivity (Denmark): home12.inet.tele.dk/fil
  This website is a hub of Philosophy for Children resources, including information on different philosophers and philosophical stories.
- Philosopher's Island: Middleton Cheney Primary School: www.portables2.ngfl.gov.uk/pmpercival/philosophy
  This site allows you to enter a narrative in which you have to develop your own philosophical responses to the situation depicted.
- Philosophy & The Enquiring Child: www.creative-corner.co.uk/schools/tuckswood/Philosophy/index.html
  This site is one school's attempt to provide a broad array of philosophical activities available for young children.
- Philosophy by Topic: users.ox.ac.uk/~worc0337/phil_topics.html#children
  This Web page contains a list of resources grouped by region; it is part of a larger site.

REFERENCES

Aristotle. 1999. *The Nichomachean Ethics*. Trans. Terence Irwin. 2nd ed. Indianapolis, IN: Hackett Publishers.

Barclay, William, ed. 2002. *Letters to the Corinthians*. 3rd ed. Louisville, KY: Westminster John Knox Press.

Baum, L. Frank. 2000. *The Wonderful Wizard of Oz*. New York: HarperCollins.

Brown, Margaret Wise. 1990. *The Important Book*. New York: HarperCollins.

Catalanotto, Peter. 2001. *Emily's Art*. New York: Atheneum Books.

Cathcart, Thomas, and Daniel Klein. 2007. *Plato and a Platypus Walk into a Bar . . . : Understanding Philosophy through Jokes*. New York: Harry N. Abrams.

Cowhey, Mary. 2006. *Black Ants and Buddhists: Thinking Critically and Teaching Differently in the Primary Grades*. Portland, ME: Stenhouse Publishers.

Descartes, René. 1993. *Meditations on First Philosophy*. Trans. Donald A. Cress. 3rd ed. Indianapolis, IN: Hackett Publishers.

Fisher, Robert. 2008. *Teaching Thinking*. 3rd ed. New York: Continuum.

Frege, Gottlob. 1960. *Translations from the Philosophical Writings of Gottlob Frege*. Trans. Peter Geach and Max Black. Oxford: Blackwell.

Freire, Paulo. 1970. *Pedagogy of the Oppressed*. Trans. Myra Bergman Ramos. New York: Herder and Herder.

Gaarder, Jostein. 1991. *Sophie's World*. New York: Berkley Books.

Kennedy, David. 1996. "Forming Philosophical Communities of Inquiry in Early Childhood Classrooms." *Early Childhood Development and Care* 120: 1–15.

———. 2006. *The Well of Being: Childhood, Subjectivity, and Education*. Albany, NY: SUNY Press.

Kidder, Tracy. 1989. *Among Schoolchildren*. New York: Harper.

Linkletter, Art. 1957. *Kids Say the Darndest Things!* Englewood Cliffs, NJ: Prentice-Hall.

Lionni, Leo. 1967. *Frederick*. New York: Pantheon.

Lipman, Matthew. 2003. *Thinking in Education*. 2nd ed. New York: Cambridge University Press.

Lobel, Arnold. 1999. *Frog and Toad Together*. New York: HarperCollins.

Matthews, Gareth B. 1980. *Philosophy and the Young Child*. Cambridge, MA: Harvard University Press.

———. 1984. *Dialogues with Children*. Cambridge, MA: Harvard University Press.

———. 1994. *The Philosophy of Childhood*. Cambridge, MA: Harvard University Press.

Nagel, Thomas. 1987. *What Does It All Mean?* Oxford: Oxford University Press.

Palmer, Donald. 1994. *Looking at Philosophy: The Unbearable Heaviness of Philosophy Made Light*. Mountain View, CA: Mayfield.

Plato. 1961. *The Collected Dialogues of Plato*. Ed. Edith Hamilton and Huntington Cairns. Princeton, NJ: Princeton University Press.

Quine, Willard Van Orman. 1960. *Word and Object*. Cambridge, MA: MIT Press.

———. 1961. *From a Logical Point of View*. 2nd ed. Cambridge, MA: Harvard University Press.

Steig, William. 1973. *The Real Thief*. New York: Square Fish.

Rawls, John. 1971. *A Theory of Justice*. Cambridge, MA: Harvard University Press.

Silverstein, Shel. 1964. *The Giving Tree*. New York: HarperCollins.

Willems, Mo. 2004. *Knuffle Bunny: A Cautionary Tale*. New York: Hyperion Books.

Wiseman, Bernard. 1989. *Morris the Moose*. New York: Harper and Row.

Wittgenstein, Ludwig. 1953. *The Philosophical Investigations*. Trans. G. E. M. Anscombe. New York: MacMillan. (Orig. pub. 1950.)

11046819R0

Made in the USA
Lexington, KY
06 September 2011